Like *Smart Work, Smart Te*  accelerate and step-change y productive team is so critica of the way we work, with diverse teams in diverse environments. Dermot has again provided a brilliant, practical and insightful way to take your team or organisation to another level.

— **Mark Bateson,** Operations Director, Miele Australia

Dermot's work on personal productivity has had a significant impact on my ability to stay organised and in control in a fast-paced and agile work environment. *Smart Teams* is packed with practical tools and techniques you can use right now to lead more effective and collaborative teams ... essential reading for those that want to expand their leadership impact.

— **Richard Burns,** General Manager, Customer Experience & Technology, Aussie Home Loans

The saying 'if you want to go fast go alone, but if you want to go far go together' echoes through this great book. Personal productivity is like learning to walk, team productivity is like learning to run.

— **Matt Church,** Founder, Thought Leaders Global and author of *Amplifiers*

Dermot Crowley is Australia's leading thinker and writer in the domain of productivity. His first book, *Smart Work,* taught us how to work productively in the digital age. *Smart Teams* is a breakthrough body of work that teaches us how to create cultures of productivity in our teams and organisations. Implementing the strategies around meetings will give you your life back, and the rest of the book will transform the impact of your team and business. Critical reading for anyone who wants their team to be more effective.

— **Peter Cook,** author of *The New Rules of Management*

Smart Teams is perfect for the clever and busy professional who wants to help create flow rather than friction. It is packed full of practical advice to not only increase your own productivity but to create a superproductive culture. This book is a must-read for anyone in corporate trying to do more with less.

—**Gabrielle Dolan,** author of *Stories for Work:*
The Essential Guide to Business Storytelling

In *Smart Teams,* Dermot Crowley takes the individual productivity concepts introduced in *Smart Work* to an entirely different level. The game theory productivity concept is brilliant, illustrating how to work with others in a way that enhances not only your own productivity, but that of the entire team. This book is an invaluable resource, filled with practical insights and ideas for immediate implementation to improve organisational productivity.

—**Chris Galloway,** Managing Director,
Morningstar Investment Management, Asia Pacific

In business today, productivity growth is fundamental. Dermot Crowley's first book, *Smart Work,* is an incredible asset for every individual—a must read. With *Smart Teams,* Dermot has done it again. He is skilled at creating simple, practical illustrations and instructions that bring to life the opportunities and solutions for teams to become more productive and for their organisations to grow as a result. Find time to read it.

—**David Smith,** Managing Director, Diageo Australia

The Smart Work approach to personal productivity helped myself and my team to claw back some time and sanity. *Smart Teams* will now allow us to go to the next level and create a culture where productivity can flourish. A smart book that is relevant to any busy team in the modern workplace.

—**Angus Sullivan,** Executive General Manager, Retail Sales &
Service, Commonwealth Bank of Australia

SMART TEAMS

SMART

COMMUNICATE, CONGREGATE, COLLABORATE

TEAMS

HOW TO WORK
BETTER TOGETHER

DERMOT CROWLEY

BEST-SELLING AUTHOR OF *SMART WORK*

WILEY

First published in 2018 by John Wiley & Sons Australia, Ltd
42 McDougall St, Milton Qld 4064

Office also in Melbourne

Typeset in 11/13pt ITC Berkeley Oldstyle Std

© John Wiley & Sons Australia, Ltd 2018

The moral rights of the author have been asserted

A catalogue record for this book is available from the National Library of Australia

Microsoft, Project, Office, OneNote, Outlook, Planner, PowerPoint, Excel and Windows are either registered trademarks or trademarks of Microsoft Corporation in the United States and/or other countries. All other trademarks are the property of their respective owners.

Cover design by Wiley

Internal illustrations by Michael Fink

'Principles in action' illustration: © ulimi/iStockphoto

Printed in Singapore by C.O.S. Printers Pte Ltd

10 9 8 7 6 5 4 3 2 1

Disclaimer
The material in this publication is of the nature of general comment only, and does not represent professional advice. It is not intended to provide specific guidance for particular circumstances and it should not be relied on as the basis for any decision to take action or not take action on any matter which it covers. Readers should obtain professional advice where appropriate, before making any such decision. To the maximum extent permitted by law, the author and publisher disclaim all responsibility and liability to any person, arising directly or indirectly from any person taking or not taking action based on the information in this publication.

CONTENTS

ABOUT THE AUTHOR

Dermot Crowley's passion is productivity. He makes dealing with schedules, priorities, technology, projects, plans and productive cultures not only simple and practical, but also fun. That's how he delivers results in the modern workplace.

He has more than twenty years' experience in the productivity training industry where he has worked as an author, speaker, trainer and thought leader. He has run his own business, Adapt Productivity, since 2002. He is also the author of *Smart Work*, published by John Wiley in 2016.

Dermot was born in Dublin, Ireland, and moved in 1993 to Sydney, Australia, where he now lives a ridiculously balanced life, spending way too much time watching and playing sport, hill climbing and drinking good coffee.

www.dermotcrowley.com.au

ACKNOWLEDGEMENTS

Book number two, like the dreaded second album, has been both incredibly fulfilling and more than a little challenging. Could I do it again? Was I a one-hit wonder? Was *Smart Work* even a hit? All of those doubts crept in at night, but of course there were lots of people behind the scenes to support me and keep me on track.

First, a huge thank you to my family, who support me and create the space for me to do audacious things like write books. Finn, you inspire me and give my life meaning. Here's to many more mountains to climb!

To my family in Ireland. Not quite James Joyce, but not bad for a Dub! Thank you, Donal and Margaret, for always believing in me and talking me up to all at home.

To Vera, who has helped me to believe in the positive power of my message. You reflect the best version of me. Thank you.

To my team at Adapt — Tony, Chauntelle and Matt. I look forward to bringing *Smart Teams* to life with all of you. Thank you for supporting me while I wrote it.

To all of the Thought Leaders family. I am constantly inspired and driven by your amazing company. A special mention to my mentors, Matt and Pete. I would never have started this journey without your encouragement. Matt, focus is coming!

A big thank you to all of the amazing experts who contributed to this book through interviews. It was a blast, and I learned so much. Thank you, Colin, Matt, Donna, Lynne, Harley, Paul, Scott and Stephen.

Finally, to my Smart Support Team. Thank you to Kelly for project managing me and helping me transform a pile of rubbish into an elegant state. To the team at Wiley, thank you for trusting me again. Chris and Jem, it was great to work with you again. You make my words better. And to Lucy, who fought hard for a great idea.

And mostly, thanks to you, the reader. That you have invested your money and time in my words is humbling. I hope you find the return is great.

HOW TO USE THIS BOOK

Like *Smart Work*, this book has been written with a practical focus. I want you and your team to do something different after reading this. I am sure you have the same aspirations, but I am also sure this is not the first business book you have bought. Did you implement your learnings from those other books as well as you had hoped? Maybe not. So here is my advice on implementing *Smart Teams* and starting to turn around your experience with the issues we will discuss.

Read it cover to cover, or flick through to the sections that grab your interest. Then try to identify the productivity issue that, if resolved, would have the greatest positive impact for your team. Focus on that first, and create a project to implement it straight away.

In chapters 2 and 3, I outline a process to help you and your team to decide on the most impactful productivity principles to focus on when working together. Make the time to do this exercise—it will have a real impact. In chapter 9, I propose a range of simple projects that you could implement with your team over the next couple of months to create and sustain change. I don't ask you to do them all—just pick one and implement it.

You will invest precious time and energy in reading this book. I know that is hard when you are so busy. You will then need to invest time working with your team to improve how you communicate, congregate and collaborate. Again, not easy when you are busy. But that is the point. You need to spend time to make time! Don't waste the initial time spent reading this book by doing nothing with it.

Buying this book was your first investment. Reading it your second. But implementing the recommended projects will be your third and most lucrative investment.

INTRODUCTION

Since publishing *Smart Work* I have had many conversations with clients about the best way to increase productivity across a whole team, or across an entire organisation. Individually, they loved the *Smart Work* approach, but they wanted to apply the concepts in a sustained way to *everyone* involved. This is far more complex than helping an individual increase their personal productivity.

Helping individuals to work more productively through a set of systems, processes and habits is a crucial starting point for increased team productivity. But to boost productivity across many workers in a sustained way we need to go beyond personal productivity and examine how we *work together*.

We need to look closely at how leaders, managers and team members communicate, congregate and collaborate, and ensure that everyone understands the impact that our poor work behaviours have on others' productivity. Finally, our leaders take responsibility to create a culture and an environment that will allow productivity to flourish in the long term.

No matter how great our personal productivity, and how good our intentions, every time we interact with others there is a risk that we will drag their productivity down, or that they will drag ours down.

This happens because we are busy, under pressure, tired and sometimes a bit lazy. We don't intentionally set out to hijack or kill our colleagues' productivity. Our work is complex, and we are human. And as we push hard to achieve our goals and deal with the everyday issues that come our way, we can leave a trail of collateral damage in our wake.

Can you relate?

I saw this first hand at an off-site team day for one of my key tech clients last year. I was presenting to the leadership team and their top 60 managers. I had been working with the executive team for several months, and this was the start of an initiative to drive the productivity principles to the next level.

It being a tech company, they all received a high volume of email. Most managers were getting 300 to 400 (some over 500) emails per day. This ludicrous volume of email was causing stress, missed deadlines and lots of rework, and was diverting the managers from the important work they should have been focusing on.

Midway through my presentation, their CEO stood up and asked, 'How many of you feel like you are getting hammered by emails?' Almost everyone put their hand up.

So the CEO said, 'Think about this. Last month we were all at the half-yearly conference for three days. How many of you noticed that our email volume dropped to about a third of the normal level over those three days?' Again, most raised their hand. 'Okay,' he said, 'Connect the dots for me. What happened there?'

Finally, someone in the audience said, 'We were all in a room together, so we weren't sending emails to each other. So our email volume fell.' The penny dropped for everyone in the room: when it came to email volume, they were creating their own problems.

In their heads, they had been blaming external forces—their US head office, customers, suppliers. Everyone but themselves. But the reality was that they themselves had created an email culture that had gone wild.

Email was the preferred communication method, even to the person at the next desk. Everyone was CC'd on everything. 'Reply All' conversations were rife, sometimes generating 30 to 40 emails for each individual, even though the conversations were relevant to few of them. No wonder their inboxes were overflowing!

Many of those managers had already implemented the *Smart Work* system to manage their own productivity, but how could they possibly keep up when faced with the deluge of emails in their inboxes each day? How could they be expected to focus on the right stuff when they were drowning in the wrong stuff?

Personal productivity training was a part of the solution, but the greater need for the group was a shift in culture. A move away from the rampant email culture that had evolved over the years to one that used email in a more thoughtful way. A shift away from the 'death by meeting' culture to a more balanced one, with fewer meetings, involving fewer people, taking less time and achieving better outcomes. A shift away from a culture of complicated collaboration that just frustrated people, to one where great things were achieved when they worked together.

Having said that, this was a highly successful global organisation, so they must have been doing lots right. And they were. They got stuff done. But the costs of a less-than-effective productivity culture were high, including long hours, stress, lack of balance and high turnover.

The culture of our team and organisation often works against our efforts to be productive — and our leaders can be a part of the problem.

Productivity problems at the team level

Smart Teams is not about task lists or zero inboxes. While these are critical at the individual level, they are not the focus here. This book looks at how we can work *together* to solve the common issues that challenge our productivity daily.

There are four key productivity issues that we face when we work together in complex environments such as the modern corporate office.

1. Information overload

Hopefully you are not dealing with the extreme volumes of email faced by the managers in the earlier story, but I bet you are not too far from this! How many emails do you get each day? Fifty or sixty? Not too bad. One hundred? That is a bit harder to manage. Two hundred? Now you are feeling the pressure. More than that and you are officially drowning!

What started out as a simple, useful communication tool between academics has become a nightmare for many workers today. Don't get me wrong, I love email—just not too much of it. And it is not just email that is overloading us with information. Each day we juggle numerous other information systems, including instant messaging, phone calls, voice mail, collaboration tools, customer management systems and project dashboards.

We simply have too much information these days, and it's sometimes difficult to turn this information into intelligence.

Studies have suggested that our stress levels start to elevate when we receive more than 50 emails daily—and that applies to most people I work with! We need to reduce the volume of emails and other information we send and receive. Most of it is just noise, and the signal is getting lost.

While taking advantage of the speed of communication and the easy access to information that tools such as email provide, we need to get back to a more focused way of working.

2. Too much time in unfocused meetings

Meetings are an important way for us to get work done, working with and through other people. But for some of us, especially senior managers, they have taken over our whole week, leaving us with little time to get anything else done.

These can be resource-heavy collaborations during which only one or two people in the meeting are actually doing the work, while everyone else watches on. There is an old Irish joke that sums this up well: 'How many workers does it take to dig a hole? Six. One to dig the hole and five to stand around and watch.' Meetings should not be a spectator sport. If you are not a player, should you even be there?

If not managed well, meetings can have adverse consequences. Your workday should strike a healthy balance between time working with others and time getting your own stuff done. If you are in meetings most of the day, you will have little time for your own work and your productivity will drop. When you compensate for this imbalance by working longer hours, your stress levels rise, relationships get frayed and the quality of your work drops as you miss deadlines or are constantly rushing to get stuff done on time.

Meetings often take more time than is necessary. An hour, 60 minutes, is a nice, round timeframe. But isn't 30 minutes just as neat, and potentially more productive? Parkinson's Law states that the work will always expand to fill the time available. We tend to schedule meeting durations based on habit rather than need.

Finally, most meetings are poorly planned. Too many participants come unprepared and waste everyone's time by preparing *during* the meeting. Changing this culture gives us a great opportunity to boost team productivity without too much effort.

3. Distractions and interruptions

Surely after the hours we have spent wading through those emails and listening intently in those meetings we deserve a bit of time to focus on getting some of our own work done at our desk? But no, even there we are bombarded by distractions and interruptions.

The truth is most of us are our own worst enemy here. We become victims of email, and of our teammates. We don't bother to turn off our email alerts, because we quite like to see what is coming into our overflowing inbox. We like the distraction, yet complain bitterly about it to others. We often fail to manage physical interruptions too. People interrupt us and we all too often just let it happen. So when we do have some time to focus on important tasks, we often don't take advantage of it.

4. Unnecessary urgency

Have you ever made it to the end of a busy day feeling like you never actually got near what you had set out to do? Was today filled with urgent issues, requests and interruptions? If that has become the norm for you, welcome to the club!

Many people in today's busy workplace are driven by a sense of urgency. Not by what is important, but by what is most insistent and pressing. Urgency is a great motivator to action, and many of us are geared towards this way of working, deferring important tasks until they hit a deadline and become urgent.

What worries and frustrates me more than anything is that most organisations too are driven by urgency. People often tell me they work in reactive organisations or reactive industries. And everyone accepts this as normal. It may be the current reality, but it does not have to be accepted by leadership or their teams.

In a culture that accepts urgency as the legitimate driver of work priorities, people are expected to react. And react they do—to their boss, to customers, to colleagues and to themselves. But this desire for a quick turnaround comes at a cost.

A reactive approach to work reduces the quality of our outputs, causes unnecessary stress and reduces motivation on a grand scale. Our busyness may make us feel productive, but being busy is not the same as being productive.

It is my experience that industries are not reactive by nature, and neither are organisations. It is people and their work styles that cause urgency and reactivity every day of the working week (and weekends if you are especially reactive).

We create friction rather than flow

In a typical team, wrestling with a combination of these complex productivity issues means our weekly productivity takes a massive hit.

> **_Like mountain climbers wading through heavy snow, we experience work friction rather than work flow._**

Everything is harder. Things take longer. We have to chase everything up. Rework means we get behind, which causes more urgency. And so the cycle goes on. We feel like we have no control or power to change these friction-causing factors. This is just the way it is!

There must be a better way.

The slow food movement was pioneered by Italian Carlo Petrini in 1986. Alarmed by the rise of the fast food culture, he was initially motivated by a campaign to stop the opening of a McDonald's restaurant at the foot of Rome's famous Spanish Steps. I believe we need a 'slow work' movement to create cultures that are _responsive_ rather than _reactive_.

We need to slow things down a bit, and take more control of doing good-quality work in a timely way. The irony is that by slowing down we will get more work done in less time. And by embedding this shift across our team, we will build a platform on which to create not just a productive culture, but a _superproductive_ culture.

In Part I we will look at some ways to move your team from friction to flow.

PART I

MOVING FROM FRICTION TO FLOW

In 2001, Russell Crowe starred in *A Beautiful Mind*, a film based on the life of American mathematician John Nash. A pivotal scene in the movie depicts Nash's eureka moment when developing his thinking around non-cooperative games, or what became widely known as *Nash's Equilibrium*.

I hope that John Nash, and Russell Crowe for that matter, would excuse my poor attempt to explain such a brilliant theory, but here goes.

While watching his friends jostle for position to ask a group of women to dance, it occurred to Nash that an accepted theory by the eighteenth-century economist Adam Smith was incomplete. Smith had stated that in economics the best result comes from everyone doing what is best for themselves. Nash's insight was that the best result actually comes from everyone in the group doing what is best for themselves, *and for the group*. Nash's Equilibrium became an important contribution to the field of economic game theory, which is now used in many modern applications, from online gambling to traffic flow analysis. Sadly, I believe, it resulted in none of the men getting to dance with a beautiful woman that night (at least in the movie).

So what does this part-history, part-Hollywood lesson have to do with team productivity? Well, I reckon quite a lot. This is what I call *game theory productivity*.

Our team is most productive when we work in a way that is productive for ourselves as individuals, and productive for the team as a whole.

Creating this cultural change within your team requires a shift in mindset by everyone involved. Everyone will need to challenge their current ways of working that might serve themselves but not the wider team. There is no room for selfish or selfless mindsets.

Are you selfish?

When we focus on being personally productive, but do not consider or care about the productivity of others, we are exhibiting what I call a *selfish mindset*.

We may be well organised, ruthless in our prioritisation and focus, and obsessed about working only on the key activities that help us to achieve our outcomes. But when we interface with others, we care little for how our behaviours affect their productivity.

This may mean we send rushed, poorly written emails to save ourselves time, creating extra work for others as they try to decipher our communications. Too busy working on our own important priorities to stay on top of our email, we fail to accept or decline meeting invitations. The meeting organisers, and other participants, are unsure if we are attending. This can lead to lost productivity, as when we fail to attend, the meeting wastes everyone else's time because we are needed to make the final decision!

In a senior team I once worked with, one of the directors had an interesting approach to meetings. He accepted meeting invites but would often not turn up for the meeting. Only if someone bothered to come and fetch him might he decide to wander over and grace the team with his presence.

His justification for not turning up on time would be that he was in the middle of something more important. As a senior manager, he may have been working and prioritising effectively. But as a team member, and as a leader, he was dragging down the productivity of the team, and setting a poor example.

How many people in his team would then feel it was okay to turn up to meetings late — because everyone knows it will not start on time?

In a productive team environment, we simply cannot operate with a selfish mindset.

Are you selfless?

At the other end of the continuum is what I call the *selfless mindset*. Some people go out of their way to help others to be productive, but at the expense of their own productivity.

A good example of this is people who feel the need to answer all emails the minute they arrive in their inbox. They have their

3

email alerts always turned on, so they note the arrival of each new message, whereupon they drop what they are doing to respond to the incoming request. Yes, that may keep the sender's work flowing nicely, but the distraction has a real impact on the recipient's productivity.

Another example of selflessness is people who accept every meeting invitation, without any real thought to how effective a use of their time that meeting is, or the opportunity cost to their other priorities if they attend. While working in a selfless way seems to be a noble position, what suffers in the end is your results and balance, and your stress levels.

Or do you serve?

Is there a workable middle ground? I believe so. I think that we can operate in a way that accords with the game theory principle. The best result comes from doing what is best for ourselves and for the group at the same time.

When we adopt what I call a *serving mindset*, we always try to balance our own productivity with the productivity of the team. We think on two levels, and hold these competing ideas in our mind every time we *communicate*, *congregate* or *collaborate*.

To operate with a serving mindset, we need to slow down and think when working with others. We need to operate with a mindfulness and awareness that enhances the productivity of all involved. This is not a zero-sum game — it should be a win–win.

We should take the time to help others to stay productive. The payback? If we can inspire this mindset in others, then we in turn will reap the rewards. And the productivity of the team will exponentially increase.

A serving mindset is crucial if we want to transform the friction that permeates most workplaces into flow.

1

ENABLING PRODUCTIVE FLOW

While some of our work is done alone, most of it involves working with others. When we work with others we *cooperate*, working together to achieve shared results. We commonly do this in the context of communications, meetings and projects, although we may cooperate in many other ad-hoc ways.

Our challenge is the unproductive friction we create for others when we cooperate, and of course the friction they create for us.

A good friend of mine is an experienced sailor who has competed in gruelling events such as the Sydney to Hobart Yacht Race. He knows how to make a boat go fast, and he knows what slows a boat down.

He once told me a story of how a bucket attached to a rope fell overboard during a race, causing a sudden and almost immediate drag on the boat. Now, everyone on board that racing yacht would have known the drastic impact such an accident would have on their speed, and they wasted no time in cutting it loose.

Matt went on to tell me of a more insidious form of drag when sailing: the build-up of barnacles on a boat's hull produces an uneven surface that creates friction as the hull cuts through the water. In a race this kind of drag, being more gradual, can go unnoticed until it is too late. This is why some boat owners, especially of racing yachts, can spend thousands each year having their hulls cleaned, particularly before a race.

In the modern workplace, we face similar challenges. Sometimes someone will do something that completely disrupts our productivity. For instance, our priorities and schedule for the whole day may be upended because another department needs an issue resolved urgently.

It is as though a bucket were dropped behind our boat, causing a drag that slows us down instantly.

But sometimes our productivity is disrupted in a more insidious way by a daily build-up of little things that affect our ability to work. These disruptions turn our work flow into work friction.

Few people set out to cause friction. Some might have little regard for other people's time, but most of us do our best to get our work done, and the friction we cause is simply the collateral damage of our busyness. This friction is a major productivity drain, however, and when compounded across the team, quickly adds up.

Productivity friction

So what does friction look like? And how can we turn it into flow?

Friction is the loss of productivity and effectiveness that occurs in the 'gap' between two people, as illustrated in figure 1.1. It is that brief loss of focus when we are distracted by an interruption. It is the wasted time spent in a meeting that has no agenda and no real focus. It is the frustration we feel when an urgent request derails our day and the priorities we had planned. It is the sense of overwhelm we feel every time we open our inbox to find hundreds of new messages waiting for our attention.

None of these issues are major problems in themselves, but over days and weeks they add up to create a friction that makes our work harder than it needs to be.

Figure 1.1: friction versus flow

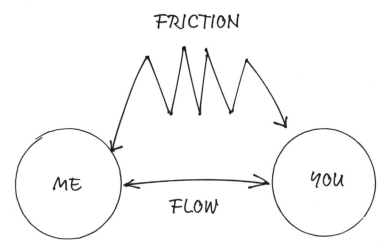

FRICTION: Negatively affecting the productivity of others through lack of awareness or lack of care.

FLOW: Consciously working to enhance our own productivity as well as the productivity of those around us.

Poor productivity behaviours

In a team where friction rules, you will find the following behaviours affecting the productivity of all concerned:

Meetings

- Participants turn up late to meetings.

- Participants arrive unprepared.

- The wrong people are invited.

- They fail to follow through on agreed actions.

- Meetings are called at short notice.

- Meeting agendas and outcomes are fuzzy.

Emails

- We send too many emails.
- Our communications are not expressed clearly.
- The desired actions are buried in the body.
- We copy people into the email unnecessarily.
- We write fuzzy subject lines.
- Every email is marked 'urgent'.

Delegation

- We choose the wrong people for the job.
- We delegate at the last minute.
- We don't take the time to delegate well.
- We delegate all responsibility but no power.
- We micromanage the delegation.
- We don't provide enough support when needed.

Interruptions

- We make too many interruptions.
- We show a lack of awareness and empathy.
- We interrupt just because we have a thought.
- We make negotiation hard for the other person.
- We make every interruption an urgent issue.

Deadlines

- We leave work tasks until the last minute.
- We create unnecessary urgency.
- We expect instant responses.
- We forget or fail to meet deadlines.

All of these examples of poor productivity behaviour cause friction, not just between two individuals, but across the team.

If we do not manage it, friction will pile on top of friction. What if we could reduce the friction that occurs when we work with others? We probably cannot totally eradicate it, but if we reduced it just a little in every interaction, and we did this across our whole team, the productivity gain would be huge.

In his book *Will It Make the Boat Go Faster?*, British rower Ben Hunt-Davis talks about 'the aggregation of marginal gains', a concept he learned from the British Cycling performance director David Brailsford. This idea suggests that 1 per cent improvements in different areas such as training, diet and aerodynamics would aggregate to a massive overall performance improvement.

If we were to reduce the productivity friction in many areas of our work, such as our emails, our meetings and our project collaborations, we would enjoy a massive increase in productivity. And if we did this consistently across the team, we would create a more productive culture — a culture where flow was the norm.

Friction vs flow cultures

Running through my son's recent end-of-term report, I noticed he was marked as late on several days over the term. For me this was unacceptable. His response was, 'But Dad, all my friends are late more often than I am!' In my head, I recalled much the same conversation with my own parents, and my reply to my son was very similar to theirs: 'I don't care what your friends do. This is my expectation of you ...'

In the workplace, our productivity behaviours cannot be measured against the group norm. Just because most people are late to meetings does not make it okay. We need to measure ourselves against a higher standard, one that is not diminished by group behaviours.

The group norm must not dictate our behaviours.
Our behaviours must dictate the group norm.

The culture of a team is partly dictated by the behaviours and habits of the individuals in that team. In a friction culture, poor productivity behaviours across the team cause disruption rather than collaboration. The common feeling is of 'busyness'.

In a flow culture, on the other hand, people don't talk about how busy they are. We are all busy. Move on. They instead talk about how *productive* they are, even if their schedule is full. (When people ask me if I am busy at the moment, I now refuse to say 'yes,' replying instead, 'No, my schedule is productively full.' This is not just about positive spin. It is about mindset.)

Many friction cultures feel like they are always short on resources. There is much talk about how short-staffed we are, how we have too much to do and not enough time, so we can't get *anything* done. Sound familiar?

In flow cultures, we not only use our time more effectively because we are organised, focused and proactive, but we get more done because we are resourceful. We find a way. We work it out. We are in control of getting what is important done on time.

How do we move from a friction culture to a flow culture?

Beyond personal productivity

Increased productivity, especially sustained increased productivity, does not just happen by itself. Productivity must be led by leaders who make it a priority, and who passionately lead by example so their team model their way of working.

For greatest impact and leverage, leaders and managers at all levels in the business should put the productivity of their team on the agenda, and make it a personal priority to support and lead the productivity effort.

Cultures are formed around a set of principles and behaviours that are modelled by everyone, starting with the leadership team. If your work style is reactive, disorganised and chaotic, the culture of your organisation will mirror this.

As a leader, you have an opportunity to boost the productivity of those around you, and to set up your organisation for many years of sustained productivity.

Over the past 15 years I have worked in many organisations, helping individuals and teams to improve their personal productivity. I am passionate about this work but have been frustrated at times by how great training and coaching can be undone by the culture of an organisation.

I believe that this applies especially to productivity training. Individuals come back from a training day fired up, excited about the potential of their new learnings, and ready to change the habits of a lifetime. But for all their efforts to work more proactively, the reactive culture they work in drags them back into firefighter mode, reacting to urgency and putting out fires.

For all their desire to get to the impactful work in their role, their time is squandered dealing with operational issues, often caused by someone else's poor work practices or lack of planning. Even with the best intentions to create space for the important work, their time is taken up with endless meetings and a deluge of emails.

Research by Bain & Company has confirmed how culture can work against the good intentions of workers and teams. One report on large organisations found the problem to be cultural as much as systemic, with the corporate culture tending to siphon resources away from externally focused, customer-serving tasks. The report noted:

> *Most time management advice focuses on individual actions— be choosy with meetings, rein in your email box. But this advice sometimes goes against your company's culture: Ignore emails and meeting invitations and you risk alienating your colleagues—or your boss.*

Figure 1.2 (overleaf) outlines the different productivity cultures that can exist, and what needs to happen for an organisation to move up the ladder from *disruptive* to *superproductive*.

Figure 1.2: from disruptive to superproductive

PRODUCTIVITY CULTURE	BEHAVIOUR IN ORGANISATION	IMPACT
SUPERPRODUCTIVE	Build a productivity culture	SUSTAINED
Inspire culture ↑		
COLLABORATIVE	Facilitate team productivity	LEVERAGED
– – Champion protocols ↑ – – – – – – – – – – – – – – – – – –		
PRODUCTIVE	Develop personal productivity	ENHANCED
Develop skills ↑		
PASSIVE	Tolerate poor productivity	IGNORED
Raise awareness ↑		
DISRUPTIVE	Cause disrupted productivity	SABOTAGED

Level 1: DISRUPTIVE

Many leadership teams talk about the importance of productivity in the organisation, yet the truth is they are sometimes a part of the problem. While they may have the best interests of staff at heart, sometimes the ever-changing environment and the constant pressure to achieve results lead to behaviours that have a negative effect on productivity. This can lead to a reactive culture with fuzzy priorities and little support to help people to work in a productive way.

Everyone works long hours to deal with their massive workload, lurching from one urgent issue to another, drowning in email and back-to-back meetings.

If this is the culture in which we work, we need to raise awareness and set some expectations about how the team could operate to ensure maximum productivity. This is especially critical at the leadership level, as poor productivity behaviours can have a doubly negative effect. If the leadership team's mindset is off, you can expect that their teams will adopt a similar mindset. As the comedian Eddie Murphy used to observe, 'Follow a stupid kid home, and I bet your bottom dollar you will find stupid parents.'

Level 2: PASSIVE

In some organisations, a passive culture predominates. The leadership team may not be causing the productivity issues, but they also may not be doing enough to protect their teams from them. They may ignore the need to work on productivity, and believe they can get by using outdated methods and cobbled-together organising systems.

They may still use obsolete tools to organise themselves, and personally resist the adoption of technology to boost productivity. Perhaps they see the benefit for others but convince themselves that they don't need to change and are operating just fine with the toolkit they have built for themselves over the years.

The key to reaching the next level is to make productivity a priority, and to take steps to upgrade the personal productivity skills of everyone in the team. This is where personal productivity training comes in, and it is this training that makes up much of the work I have done historically with my clients. But, as we will discuss, personal productivity training fixes only part of the productivity problem.

Level 3: PRODUCTIVE

At the productive level, leadership may have invested time and money to develop the skills of the team and achieve enhanced productivity. But here is the real challenge, and the real opportunity. If we stop here, as I believe most organisations do, the productivity gain may be limited, as the efficiencies gained by the individual are offset by the friction caused by our co-workers.

So the next focus needs to be on agreeing on and embracing a set of productivity principles that, when adopted by the team, serve to enhance team productivity. When we operate according to a set of agreed behaviours every time we *communicate, congregate* and *collaborate*, our collective productivity cannot help but increase. This reduces friction and increases flow.

Level 4: COLLABORATIVE

For the organisation that goes from productive to collaborative, work will flow, with the effectiveness of the team increasing in a highly leveraged way. The sum is greater than the parts.

But adopting a set of agreed protocols can generate an initial flurry of excitement and action that soon recedes as we fall back into our old habits. They become posters on the wall that we don't even notice anymore. If this happens, the productivity gain at the collaboration level can be short-lived. The final focus on the journey to creating a superproductive organisation requires a long-term change in culture.

We need leaders at all levels to step up and champion this new way of working to achieve sustained productivity. If we stick with it, the culture will change for the better, and over time even new starters will quickly begin to operate productively in their new superproductive workplace.

Level 5: SUPERPRODUCTIVE

Superconductors, like those used in MRI machines, operate at extremely low temperatures and can reduce the energy lost to resistance enormously. In fact, a current in a superconducting circuit can theoretically travel around the circuit for decades without loss of power. The lack of resistance ensures the purity of the energy.

Similarly, a superproductive culture can experience a sustained increase in productivity across the team or organisation, and will ensure the energy of the workers is maximised. Everyone works in a way that is personally productive, but also productive for those around them. And the culture ensures that these mindsets become a part of the DNA of the organisation.

A superproductive organisation not only experiences very high levels of productivity across the team, but ensures this productivity gain is sustained over time, even when members of the team leave and new members join. Superproductive becomes 'the way we work around here'.

Imagine a culture in which everyone is highly skilled at managing their time and priorities.

Imagine a culture in which people actively work to enhance their own productivity as well as the productivity of others.

Imagine a culture in which productivity is embedded in the DNA of the organisation.

So how do we move to this ultimate level of productivity? How do we inspire a culture that will allow productivity to flourish? Let us look at the pathway to reducing friction and enabling productive flow.

2

QUALITIES OF A SMART TEAM

Whatever your favourite sport, I am sure you will recognise the value of the good 'team player'. Someone who goes beyond personal glory for the good of the team, who makes their teammates look good. A player who always works tirelessly to get the result the team needs.

No doubt your colleagues work hard at being team players. I truly believe that most of us want to do our jobs to the best of our ability, and to support each other to deliver outcomes.

But when it comes to productivity, sometimes we let the team down. We don't mean to, but we get busy, stressed, overwhelmed, and it all starts to slip a bit. This is where a *smart team player* steps up to support the rest of the team from a productivity perspective. (To be clear, 'smart' here has nothing to do with intelligence; it refers, rather, to a team that has evolved a different, more effective way of working.)

To build a smart team, we need to get everyone on the same page, so we all agree on what productive behaviours would look like. This shared understanding will help your team to practise the right behaviours and to cooperate in a way that creates flow.

To work productively as a smart team, each team member needs to review and be prepared change their behaviours.

The starting point for this is to explore the qualities that a smart team player models.

While a smart team player has many qualities that make them excellent at their job, there are four qualities that have a direct impact on team productivity.

A smart team player is:

1. *purposeful*. They work with purpose on the right activities.

2. *mindful*. They are mindful of how their behaviours affect others.

3. *punctual*. They turn up on time, and deliver on time.

4. *reliable*. They do what they say they will do.

Figure 2.1 outlines the four key qualities of the smart team player.

Figure 2.1: smart team qualities

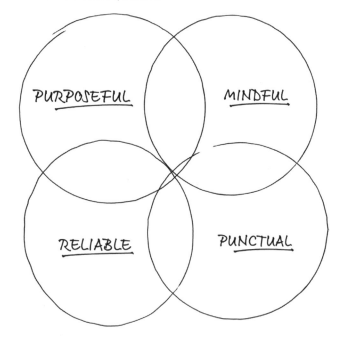

We are purposeful

When we embrace the idea of working with purpose, we strive to always work on the things that have an impact in our role. We are clear about our priorities and the priorities of the team, and are not overly distracted by urgency or busywork.

We work with clear intent, and always manage our schedule, our time, our relationships and even our inbox with purpose.

Working with purpose requires a clear sense of our objectives and priorities. If we understand only vaguely what our role is, and are not crystal clear about what we should be focused on, it is very easy to become distracted by shiny, glittery activities that hold no real value.

Sadly, I believe that many of us have to some degree lost our sense of purpose at work. Rather than being driven by what is important, we are pressured into responding to our emails and what is urgent. We are always busy, but busyness is not enough in a high-performing team. As Henry David Thoreau once said, 'It is not enough to be busy. So are the ants. The question is: What are we busy about?'

Successful companies such as Amazon, Apple and Atlassian have one thing in common (besides starting with the letter A). They build teams that have a strong sense of purpose, which drives everything they do, including their productivity. They put a lot of effort into creating that shared purpose, and in attracting people who have this quality.

We are mindful

Mindfulness has become a popular buzzword in today's distracted workplace. There are many books and courses on how to practise mindfulness. More often than not, their interpretation of mindfulness is focused inward—on awareness of what is happening with your own attention and focus. This is essential if you want to be productive in an email-heavy, interruption-driven workplace.

A second interpretation of mindfulness has an outward focus. Mindfulness makes us more aware of what is happening around us, and allows us to focus on the needs of those with whom we cooperate.

When we are mindful, we are thinking about how our behaviours affect other people's productivity, and we therefore try to act in a way that minimises friction for them.

This quality is the embodiment of game theory productivity, as it helps us to behave in a way that serves both ourselves and the group. We know the best result comes from our being personally productive at the same time as helping the team to be productive.

Unfortunately, a lack of mindfulness is demonstrated in workplaces every day. We generate volumes of noise for our colleagues. We are distracted in meetings. We rush work, make mistakes and end up creating more work for ourselves and others. We should approach every interaction in a mindful way. We need to slow down, and focus on what we are doing *at this moment* to save everyone time in the long run.

We are punctual

Punctuality should be non-negotiable. We should always strive to be on time, and should be held to account if we are not. This applies to more than just meetings. We need to be punctual with the delivery of our work, with responses to email requests and with returning text messages and phone calls.

Turning up and delivering on time requires us to work proactively and not leave things until the last minute. We need to have a solid action management system in place to allow us to manage our time and priorities effectively. A paper to-do list will no longer cut it — a more sophisticated and relevant approach is required here.

Whether communicating with others, congregating in meetings or collaborating on projects, we must strive always to be on time.

We need to hold ourselves to account at the highest level. It is too easy to let ourselves off the hook because we have too much to do, too many meetings, with no space to plan or think. Being on time is a mindset. People who adopt this mindset tend to be on time whatever work pressures they face.

A good friend, Oscar, who is an ex–Microsoft executive, told me the story of his first boss at Microsoft. He was ex-navy, and made it very clear to Oscar that he expected team members to turn up to every meeting five minutes before it was due to start. 'In the navy,' he told him, 'the ship departs at 8 am. If you arrive after that, the ship has sailed.'

This naval view was very black and white: if you were late, the ship sailed without you, and that had real consequences and penalties. This is a great discipline, and when practised consistently it becomes a non-negotiable quality.

We are reliable

I often see people falling victim to their schedule, their priorities and their inbox. They complain about how busy they are, but do not take adequate steps to prioritise or manage their work effectively. To be a reliable team member, you must be in control of your work and accountable for what you deliver. That means you also need to take responsibility for saying 'no' and negotiating your workload when appropriate.

We must take ownership and be accountable for our work, our deadlines and our promises.

Taking ownership is critical in a productive team, and is valued by leaders, managers and colleagues alike. It requires a 'do what you say' mindset, and an organised approach to our work.

We want to work with people we can trust, people who have our back. As managers, we don't have time to be constantly chasing our team for work, or fixing avoidable mistakes that were caused by a lack of accountability.

I recently presented at a conference for a major client in the mortgage industry. When my session finished, I found I still had an hour before the car was to pick me up to go to the airport. So I decided to sit in on the end-of-day presentation on the main stage.

The speaker was Ben Roberts-Smith, a former Australian SAS soldier and the most highly decorated soldier of his generation in the Commonwealth. His stories were an inspiration, and provided a wonderful template for leadership in any workplace. The part that really stood out for me was when he talked about his actions when under enemy fire.

He said that what made it easy, or at least easier, for him to be courageous in a life-threatening situation was the fact that he trusted his team and knew he could rely on them in any situation. They all operated according to a strong set of personal and professional values, and they absolutely did what they said they would do. He did things that put his life at risk to protect his teammates, and he knew they would do the same for him without question.

We might not be facing the same life-or-death situations as Ben and his comrades, but we still can and should work in such a way that our team can rely on us absolutely.

3

CHANGING TEAM BEHAVIOURS

So, what would be the benefit for our team if we operated according to this set of qualities at work? We all know we should do the right thing, but when we are busy and under pressure it can be difficult. Your team will need to understand a clear benefit before they put the effort into adopting these qualities. But once they are on board, how will they change behaviours in a consistent way?

Figure 3.1 (overleaf) shows how the four qualities of a smart team combine to deliver powerfully productive outcomes.

When we are *purposeful* and *mindful*, we create incredible **focus**, as we work on high-impact activities, and manage both our internal attention and the external awareness of those around us. This is of great benefit in a modern workplace that is so often driven by distraction and interruption.

When we are *mindful* and *punctual* we ensure that we treat our colleagues with **respect**. We are aware of how our behaviours affect their productivity, and we do them the courtesy of turning up and delivering on time. This in turn builds respect with our colleagues.

Punctuality and *reliability* ensure we build **trust** with our co-workers and clients. They know they can depend on us. They don't have to spend additional time or energy chasing us or stressing that we won't deliver what they need in a timely way.

Figure 3.1: smart team outcomes

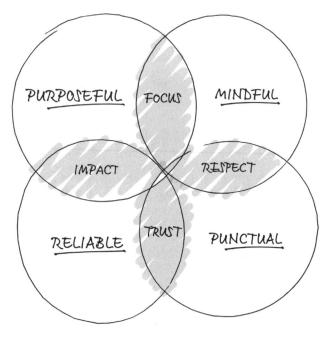

Finally, when we are *reliable* and *purposeful*, we create **impact**. We go beyond day-to-day busyness to deliver work that makes a difference. This not only motivates us, but also makes our team look and feel good. When we work with these qualities front and centre in our mind, we create the outcomes of focus, respect, trust and impact.

This is a simple but powerful combination and, once embedded in your team, will remove a lot of the friction that can drain your productivity when you work together. These will help you to do the right thing, whatever the situation, as Ben Roberts-Smith and his team demonstrated.

The four smart team qualities provide a broad framework for the team to think about how they should behave. But we need to get more specific if we really want to create a lasting change to the culture of our team. Keeping these four qualities in mind, we need to combat the productivity issues we see in our workplace every day by agreeing how we will work together and interact to maximise productivity.

We need to bring these qualities and outcomes to life so they become a part of the DNA of our whole team.

Get specific to change behaviours

Agreeing to embrace a set of qualities that will drive productivity is a great starting point for your team. But stopping here creates two problems.

Firstly, these qualities provide guidance, but they do not necessarily change behaviours in a busy workplace. Secondly, the general nature of these qualities makes accountability problematic. It is hard to tell if Kathy is more or less purposeful this month compared to last month.

Trying to create a cultural change in your team simply by sharing a set of qualities is unlikely to lead to success. How do you imagine *your* team would respond in this situation? They might nod along in agreement, saying what a good idea that was … and then what? Telling your team how they should work is not enough.

To create real change, we need to go from the general to the specific. We need to develop a set of specific productivity principles that will provide clear guidance on how we work together in real situations, such as in meetings and on projects.

And we need to do this *with* our team, not *to* our team.

These productivity principles, if championed by leadership and embraced by the team, shape the culture of the team. They are not meant to be the ten commandments, and they should not be just another poster on the wall. They should live and breathe in every meeting, every interaction, every delegation, every project and every email.

We will also need to hold each other to account. These behaviours are unlikely to remain in place for any length of time if management and leadership have to 'police' the productivity principles. They don't have time for that, and frankly it should not be necessary.

In a high-performing team, we hold ourselves as much as each other to account.

Over the past 16 years I have had the pleasure of raising a fine young son. Like any teenager, Finn creates challenges for me from time to time, but for the most part he has been a joy to parent. One of the realisations his mum and I had early on was that we could not control what he did or how he acted all the time.

As he got older he went from being with us most of the time in very controlled and supervised situations, to going out with his mates at the weekend, unsupervised and in situations we had no control over.

As hard as this transition was for us, we knew we could not keep him wrapped in cotton wool. We let him go, but we trusted that we had raised him well and he would for the most part make good decisions in every situation. We had instilled in him a strong set of values and qualities, and we trusted that these would guide his decision making and actions. Fingers crossed!

In a work context, we also cannot micromanage how our team work every moment of the day. We can set expectations, but then we should leave people to get on with the job and trust that they will make good decisions, and behave in an appropriate and productive way.

In his book *The Amazon Way*, John Rossman outlines 14 principles that Jeff Bezos, Amazon's CEO, and his leadership team bring to life every day in the running of the company. Rossman suggests that the leadership team's unwavering championing of these principles is one of the reasons that Amazon is such a raging success.

With a bit of work, your team will hold each other to account, and will raise one another's expectations. If practised consistently, they will form 'the way we work around here'. New starters will notice a different way of operating when they join the team. Other teams will notice and may begin to copy and mirror your behaviours.

What is a productivity principle?

Each of the four productivity qualities defines an aspect of your approach to work. In combination, they guide how you organise yourself, how you collaborate with others and what you expect from others. But they are general in nature. They don't specify what you should do in tomorrow's meeting to ensure you and the team are maximising productivity.

Productivity **principles** *are tangible examples of a quality in action. They are clearly defined and specific to a situation. It is generally easy to tell whether or not the principle has been followed.*

Taking *punctuality* as an example, there are lots of principles that could hang off this quality. Thinking about punctuality in relation to meetings, we could agree to work in the following way:

- Turn up on time.

- Finish meetings on time.

- Deliver on meeting actions in a timely way.

- Use an agenda to manage time in a meeting.

If we were communicating a lot by email, and wanted to ensure we were working in a *mindful* way, we might apply the following concepts:

- Reduce email noise for the team.

- Copy or CC with purpose.

- Switch to a direct conversation if necessary.

- Make it easy for the reader.

The key to a useful productivity principle is that it is related to both a *quality* and a *situation*. The four qualities model provides a framework to ensure we are smart team players and is a useful structure to help us generate a set of behaviours to guide our work.

Generating principles for your team

Here I could simply list a set of principles to share with your team, but I won't—for two reasons. Every workplace is different, and every team is different. The productivity challenges that I face in my business are different from the ones your team faces each day.

There is no one-size-fits-all list of productivity principles.

While the productivity principles I could offer would all make sense to you, some would be more relevant to your team and the issues you face daily. You will not implement them if they are not that relevant.

You also need to consider ownership. If you just take on my list of behaviours, you and your team will not *own* them—you will be borrowing them from me. And in my experience we tend to look after things we own better than we do things we have borrowed.

If we create principles in consultation with our team, and set the expectation that they are encouraged by all of us rather than enforced by the boss, we build greater ownership and buy-in.

Principles in action

Qualities: *Purposeful, Mindful, Punctual, Reliable*

You will find this 'Principles in action' feature distributed at relevant points throughout the book. This feature is designed to illustrate how the principles show up in real life. It can be used by you and your team as a thought starter when generating your own set of productivity principles.

So I believe you will be better served by defining a list of agreements that address the specific productivity issues that show up regularly in your work environment.

Less is more in this situation. Too many principles will confuse everyone and be hard to implement. A few principles well executed are better than many barely executed at all.

I suggest brainstorming a list of eight to twelve productive behaviours that are most relevant for your team, then put a plan in place to bring them to life in all your interactions over the coming months. Further on, I will outline a process to facilitate the generation of your smart team's principles list.

These principles need to be discussed, demonstrated, managed, monitored and lived by everyone in the team for months before they will create the cultural change the team needs.

Flipping problems into principles

So how do we develop a set of agreements that are relevant to our environment, our work and our team? A good starting point is to identify the poor productivity behaviours currently causing friction in your team, and to flip them into productivity principles.

Imagine we are being copied in on too many emails, and this problem is causing a high level of email noise in our inboxes. We 'flip' the problem into a principle by asking, 'What team behaviour would reduce this or stop it from happening?'

The result could be the principle 'CC with purpose'. This means that when sending an email we think hard about who really needs to know. We also think about our reasons for copying someone into the email. Does it serve them or us, or neither?

This principle draws on two of the productivity qualities. We are communicating with *purpose*, and we are being *mindful* of our colleagues' productivity.

Table 3.1 (overleaf) offers some more examples of problems we might flip into principles.

Table 3.1: examples of flipped problems in meetings

Productivity problem	Productivity principle
Participants arrive late to meetings.	Arrive five minutes before meetings.
Meetings have fuzzy outcomes.	Communicate the meeting purpose.
Meetings always finish late.	Start wrap-up process with ten minutes to go.
Too many participants are involved.	List participants and reason for attendance.
People don't follow through on actions.	Clarify all actions and dates before wrapping up.

When creating productivity principles, get as specific as you can. Just flipping 'Meetings finish late' into 'Finish meetings on time' may have limited success. But agreeing to start the meeting wrap-up with ten minutes to go ensures meetings finish on time, with all the end-of-meeting housekeeping done before you leave.

Being specific makes the principle very easy to execute, and makes it easy to see when it has not been followed.

Facilitating team agreements

I have found the following process helps teams to generate a set of productivity principles that they all agree to work by. It is a great exercise for your annual or half-yearly team offsite, but it can also be completed in a couple of hours in a dedicated onsite meeting.

Step 1: Choose the right group.

You first need to bring together the right people to develop the team principles for the wider group. If you have a small team, you may choose to bring everyone together to give them all an opportunity to contribute and take ownership. In a larger team or organisation, you may need to make the process more efficient by choosing a smaller group that represents a reasonable cross-section of the overall team.

Ideally each sub-team and each type of role should be represented. Including senior management as well as support

---

staff, workers as well as team leaders, will help to provide a real picture of what is happening from a productivity perspective in all teams at all levels.

Finally, someone needs to put their hand up to facilitate the process. This probably should not be the boss, but it should be someone who has some facilitation experience. Maybe someone from HR can jump in and help.

Step 2: Set the context.

On flip charts or whiteboards make two lists. One should list the four qualities:

1. purposeful
2. mindful
3. punctual
4. reliable.

On the other, list the different ways your team tends to work together regularly. This could include physical meetings, virtual meetings, delegations, projects, emails, instant messaging (IM), phone calls or using collaboration tools, or simply through interrupting each other.

These lists will help to identify the productivity problems because they provide different perspectives. Listing the quality you want to act on and the situation in which the quality might be applied will help you to generate more ideas than if you brainstorm without these contexts.

Step 3: Brainstorm the productivity problems.

Next, brainstorm a complete list of productivity problems that you experience in your workplace regularly. This could be done as a large group, with someone listing the ideas on a flip chart, or in smaller groups that come together once the brainstorming has been done.

I am personally a fan of what is called 'silent brainstorming'. Here, everyone takes a pad of sticky notes and jots down their ideas, one per note. After ten minutes, everyone places their sticky notes on a whiteboard. If you see that someone has already covered an idea, you put your note on top of theirs.

(continued)

Facilitating team agreements (*cont'd*)

The value of this type of brainstorming is that it reduces the role of debate in the initial idea generation stage. Quieter people feel less intimidated and are less likely to have their ideas shot down, as so often happens in traditional brainstorming sessions.

The second benefit is that a stack of several notes will suggest a shared idea that is probably worth keeping. But don't discount the outliers with only one sticky note, which could include brilliant ideas that no one else has thought of.

Step 4: Narrow the problem list.

At this stage, you may have identified a lot of problems, although some will have only limited impact on your team. If you create too many principles to operate by, people won't make the necessary changes. A list of eight to twelve is probably enough to guide any team, so you may need to narrow the list down.

A good exercise here is to use what is called the MoSCoW method, developed by Dai Clegg. MoSCoW is an acronym for four prioritisation categories:

Must have. These are crucial and must be included.

Should have. These are 'nice to have' and should be included if possible.

Could have. These too are nice to have, but could be left out without any major difficulties. If you have room you might include a couple.

Would have. These are the least critical, and will probably not make the cut.

If using sticky notes, set up four flip charts to correspond to these four groups, and move the notes onto the appropriate chart. Depending on the volume, the 'Must haves' and the 'Should haves' should make the final list. You may need to discuss as a group any others that deserve to make the cut.

You should now have a focused, relevant list of productivity problems to be solved for your team!

Step 5: Flip problems to principles.

Using a whiteboard or flip chart, you can now begin the 'flipping' process. Draw a vertical line down the centre of the page, and add the column heads 'Problem' on the left and 'Principle' on the right.

Now take each problem and flip it into a tight, memorable productivity principle. Think about taking on a marketing mindset when trying to change a culture. 'CC with purpose' is so much more engaging and memorable than 'We will always think carefully about who needs to be copied in on emails', don't you think?

Step 6: Document and communicate.

Once you have flipped all of the problems, and you have compiled a list of agreements you are happy with, you now need to bring them together in a document ready for distribution. Make it look good, perhaps as a wall poster for meeting rooms, personal workstations or the canteen.

Share it with other teams. This is one way you can begin to influence the teams around you so you can work more productively with them. The more people use this, the more productive you will all be. A rising tide lifts all boats.

Make this a priority for your team

If you do nothing else after reading this book, I urge you to prioritise and invest the time in creating a list of relevant, impactful productivity principles for your team.

And this should not be a one-off exercise. Other productivity issues will crop up from time to time, so you should review this list every six to 12 months, checking that you are still following all the behaviours and whether others may need to be added.

Adopting this list will begin to change behaviours and shape the culture. But it is the exercise of coming together as a group and discussing, debating and agreeing on solutions that ensures a positive shift.

EXPERT INTERVIEW
Stephen Scott Johnson — on cultural change

I reckon I am clear about what I know, and about what I don't. I am an expert in many aspects of productivity in the workplace, but I would never claim expertise in cultural change. Yet in this book I argue that to improve productivity you must change the culture of your team!

Recognising this deficit, I decided to interview culture expert Stephen Scott Johnson, the author of *Emergent*, to talk about cultures, movements and the challenges that most organisations face when trying to implement any sort of cultural change.

I first asked Stephen why most organisations struggle to create meaningful cultural change. You might be keen to create a change to your team's productivity culture, but find that after much time and effort nothing has really changed.

Stephen believes the problem is organisations don't involve their people enough in the change process. 'They try to do change to people rather than involving people in the change. So change is something that happens from the top down.'

This is why I believe it is critical to generate your own set of productivity principles as a team. If you just distribute a list of productivity principles and dictate that this is how the team is going to work from this point forward, nothing will change. You need to involve the team and forge agreements, rather than just mandate rules or protocols.

I believe that every leadership team should aim to change the productivity culture of the entire organisation, whatever its size. The cost of poor productivity is too great *not* to do this. But I am also a realist and suspect that in most cases this cultural shift will need to happen at the team level. Team managers and leaders will need to create a more productive micro-culture within their team.

Stephen agrees with this, and indeed is convinced that this is the future of work cultures. But for it to be successful, he suggests, teams need to have a 'nested purpose'.

Organisations, particularly large organisations, are often made up of different business units or different teams, and they all have a different focus and responsibility, yet they're all part of a bigger culture. In organisations you get teams of people that work together but at the same time work alone.

So, from a productivity point of view, the sense of purpose needs to be around reducing friction and enabling everyone in the team to work as productively as possible. If you are leading a team that aspires to be superproductive, but your team functions in an environment that is likely to be disruptive or passive, you need to lead the way and shine a light for others.

The change in your team culture will inspire other teams that you work with, hopefully prompting a change in their team culture. Stephen refers to this 'ripple effect' in *Emergent*. We need to create powerful ripples.

Leadership is critical in any culture change initiative. I asked Stephen about the part played by leadership in this.

The role of leadership is to enable, and this is what leaders really struggle with. They don't know how to lead these new imperatives. It is really about empathy, and about reflection, and about these soft skills that they're not really trained in.

Leaders need to be custodians of the higher purpose of their organisation and to enable their people to actualise this purpose. To contribute, to create deeper meaning with that higher purpose. That doesn't come about by telling people how to live the purpose.

To wind up, I asked Stephen for his top three tips on creating a cultural change in a team. The first is to identify the higher purpose—from a smart teams perspective, this could be around creating flow rather than friction.

Secondly, he advocates engaging everyone in the change process. To allow them to contribute in a meaningful way to the project, and to create the space to talk about their fears and challenges as well as the positives. This is what he calls the 'shadow and light'.

Finally, he warns against 'doing' change to people. It is not a one-off thing that happens; rather, it is a series of ongoing projects that are tried and tested, and sometimes fail, but over time they lead towards a new way of working.

PART II

WORKING BETTER TOGETHER

Cooperation is defined as 'the process of working together for a common purpose or benefit'. I like this definition as it implies that we are all clear about the reason we are doing what we are doing—that is, that we are clear about our *why*.

Successful cooperation relies on asking yourself a number of questions. Productive cooperation always comes from considering first *why*, then *what*, *who*, *when* and in some cases *where* (see figure II).

Considering these questions every time you work with others on a project, call a meeting, delegate work, send an email or even interrupt someone will generate more constructive thinking and more productive interaction.

Simon Sinek, in his book *Start with Why*, makes the case that 'Why?' is the most important question for any leader who wants to motivate and inspire a team. First clarify, then communicate a clear purpose. It makes sense. We are more likely to buy into a vision, and work hard to achieve it, if we understand why we are doing it.

We are more likely to work productively with others if we uncover the *why* behind our interactions.

For example, imagine I am sitting at my desk, working on a client proposal, when I see my colleague Claire on her way to a meeting. I remember I need to check with her about some line items in the budget before the budget meeting next week. So I interrupt myself, and her, to ask her about them while it was still top of mind.

This probably sounds familiar, as it happens all the time in every workplace. But was it the most productive use of my time, or Claire's time, at that moment? Probably not. My focus on the proposal was disrupted, and Claire probably ended up being late for her meeting. If I had stopped to ask myself, 'Why am I asking this right now?', I would have had to admit that it was only because I saw Claire that I thought of it. Was it urgent? No. Could I have found a more suitable time to approach Claire? Yes.

By asking ourselves these W questions, we begin to look outwards, beyond our own selfish (or selfless) operating mindsets, to think about how our actions affect others, and to work out the best way for us to achieve our common purpose together.

Figure II: why, what, who, when and where

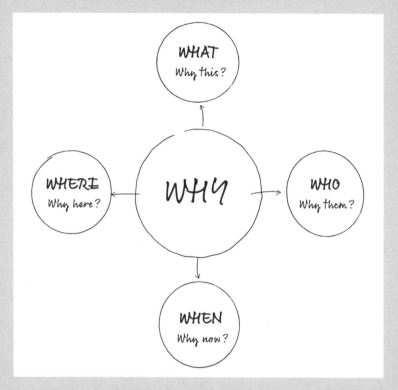

When we cooperate with others in the workplace, it is usually in one of the following situations. We are working on a project, we are in a meeting, we are interrupting someone, we are delegating work, or we are sending a written communication. Whenever we work with others, the interaction could be improved by asking the following questions.

Why this?

What outcome do you want to achieve?

To bring everyone together successfully on a project, you need to articulate clearly why the project is important. To ensure that delegated work is done to the right quality in the right timeframe, you must ensure the person delegated to understands the context of the delegation.

If you are asking six people to spend 45 minutes of their precious time in a meeting, you should invest the time in clearly outlining in the invitation why the meeting is needed. Why not only provides context; it also informs the other questions that will make the interaction successful.

Why them?

Are they the right people?

Productive collaboration also relies on working with the right people, making sure you have included the key stakeholders and not just created noise for people who do not need to be involved. This is especially true of meetings and written communication.

If you take the time to really think about who should be involved, you tend to be much more focused in your interactions, and others tend to be more open to working with you. They know their time is not going to be wasted. People like to work with organised and focused colleagues.

Why now?

Is this the best time?

Think about when. This may depend on the type of collaboration. For a project, it may involve creating a project timeline. If it is a delegation, it may involve clearly communicating a due date. If it is a meeting, it may be to identify the best time to meet, taking into account other people's schedules. With an interruption, it may be as simple as asking yourself if this is the best time to interrupt the other person.

Why here?

Is this the best place or environment?

Some interactions rely on *where* more than others, but all benefit from thinking about this in some way. If you are about to interrupt someone, it might be worth thinking about whether this is the best location, or if another environment might provide a better outcome.

When planning a project, it is worth thinking about where to store the common shared information. Once you have planned the content of a meeting, choosing an appropriate meeting space could significantly improve the meeting outcome.

Why sits at the heart of these questions, but it is asked within the context of *what*, *who*, *when* and *where*, as shown in figure II.

As we explore the three main interactions of smart teams, we will look at the way these questions help us to *communicate* with purpose and clarity, *congregate* in more impactful meetings and *collaborate* on projects more effectively.

Framing every interaction with these questions creates a powerful mindset that will ensure you and your team work together in a productive way that creates flow, rather than friction.

4

COMMUNICATE: MAKE LESS NOISE

Recently I presented at a partner conference for one of the big consulting firms. I asked the 400 partners in the room how many had more than a thousand emails in their inbox. Over 80 per cent of the room put up their hands. Overfull, poorly managed inboxes are a sure sign of a poor email culture in which not managing your inbox well is the norm.

This new reality has a direct impact on the productivity of everyone in our team, and begs the question: *Does the promise of email live up to the reality we experience today?*

It is worth thinking about the impact that email has had on our lives and how we work. Email was an amazing innovation in our workplace, increasing our ability to communicate easily with our colleagues, our clients, our friends and service providers. It is instant and inexpensive, and can travel to the other side of the world as fast as to the other side of the room.

But there is also a growing frustration with email, as our inboxes get fuller and fuller, and the volume of incoming emails per day creeps into the hundreds for some of us. Now I often have clients ask me if email is dead, or at least if it is dying. There is much discussion on the internet about the impending demise of email, and about its replacement by other, more suitable collaboration tools.

> ***The truth is, the very thing that made email so brilliant has also made it a curse: it is just too easy to use.***

Ray Tomlinson, the man credited with inventing email, did not have such problems in mind when he developed this communication tool. Like climate change, these issues are man-made. While there are some sceptics who still refute the science behind climate change, I don't think anyone would deny the problems around email use. Table 4.1 shows some ways in which the reality differs from the original promise.

Table 4.1: promise versus reality of email

Promise	Reality
Email is cheap to send.	Email costs us time.
Email supports efficiency.	Email undermines effectiveness.
It is easy to inform many.	We receive too many emails.
Information is easily disposable.	We store up emails obsessively.
24/7 communication is possible.	We recieve emails 24/7.
Distance is no barrier.	Workdays are prolonged because of different time zones.
Email supports our priorities.	Emails have become the priority.
Email makes us responsive.	Email makes us reactive.
Our inbox is always close at hand.	Our inbox is our main screen.
We have increased awareness.	We have increased noise.
We can manage our inbox.	Our inbox manages us.
Communication is stress free.	Our inbox problem is stressful.

Email overload

Email management is the number one issue that I am asked to talk about in every company I work with, at every level, from senior leadership to support staff. This is one issue that has got out of control and needs to be dealt with as a priority. There are three main ways that email overload puts us under pressure.

1. Disruption and interruption

Ten years ago, when I would ask a group of training participants how many emails they received on average each day, they would usually say about twenty to thirty. And it was killing them! That seems quaint now. Today 100 emails per day is standard for many, and several hundred the norm for senior managers or staff in some industries.

What has increased over this decade is not the number of useful, productive emails that we recieve, but the level of noise. These are emails that don't actually serve us and in fact distract us from clearly receiving the 'signal' that helps us do our jobs. Some of this noise is externally driven, but much of it comes from our colleagues and team.

One of the biggest contributors to noise is the overuse of CC and Reply All in email conversations.

These functions are generally overused, filling our inboxes with lots of information, but it's often of little value to us.

One of the strange things about emails is we tend to react to them as if they are all urgent. This is obviously not the case, yet because of the instant nature of the communication, we feel compelled to react as if they are. And this has changed the behaviour of those sending us emails. If we do not respond in a few minutes, they are calling on the phone to ask if we have seen their email yet. This is crazy!

The flood of 'urgent' emails into our inbox is a major cause of distraction and interruption.

2. Inbox bottlenecks

The never-ending flow of emails into our inboxes inevitably leads to bottlenecks. It is hard to stay on top of such a deluge, especially if we have not refined our email processing techniques. Even with our best efforts, our responsiveness suffers.

This can lead to more work, more emails and more interruptions as others chase us for the work and information they need.

> *We add to the team's urgency problems when actions are buried in our inbox, to be ignored until they become urgent enough making us then feel stressed and guilty!*

3. Stress and overwhelm

Research shows a link between email overload and stress levels. A study by Dr Thomas Jackson, in conjunction with Loughborough University, showed that while email recipients in the study were happy when they received timely information by email, they were annoyed by both irrelevant emails and emails that required an instant response. This in turn elevated their stress levels.

What can we do differently to change this current reality? What can we do to communicate in a more productive way and ease the burden of email for ourselves, our team and our colleagues? The first step may be to look at some alternatives to sending yet another email.

Be responsive, not reactive

Qualities: *Purposeful, Mindful, Punctual*

Responsiveness to email helps your team to keep work flowing. That does not mean you have to check your email every five minutes. It means you have a healthy rhythm with regard to your inbox management.

Alternatives to email

My son Finn asked me last year if I seriously got paid to help people manage email. He could not see the problem. He checked his Gmail inbox once every few weeks and rarely got anything of importance. He reasoned that executives could not find it that hard.

Then he came with me to help me set up for a presentation I was doing on a trip to London. When he heard the finance executives in the room talk about the 300-plus emails they got each day, his understanding deepened a bit. Afterwards he told me that maybe what I did was helpful after all. (Thanks mate!)

I can see his perspective. The younger generation have a different relationship to communications, and prefer to use phone-based apps to communicate with each other. Now, believe me, I reckon they have their own problems, but maybe they are not so wrong in choosing not to put all their eggs in the one basket. When it comes to communication, they use the best tool for the job, in each situation.

As the old saying goes, when you have a hammer, everything looks like a nail. When it comes to how we communicate in today's workplace, our hammer seems to be email.

You cannot completely control what other people send you, but you can influence the volume of email you receive from your team by discussing alternatives for team communication.

In fact, while you are at it, why not create some agreements about all the different modes of communication you have available? Some clarity about what communication tools to use in what situations would make everyone's life a bit easier.

Four communication tools

There are four main communication tools available for use in most organisations. Each has its place, and a context in which it is most effective (as shown in figure 4.1, overleaf). They are:

- conversation
- meeting
- email
- post.

Before we take a closer look at each, it's useful to note that both conversations and meetings are 'same time' activities. This means all parties need to do the activity in real time, at the same time. Email and posts are 'any time' activities, so the reader can read the writer's communication whenever they want to.

Conversations and posts tend to be more 'informal' in nature than some other modes of communication. Meetings and email can be seen as more 'formal' communication methods.

Figure 4.1: communication tools

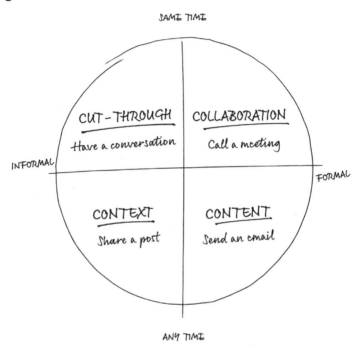

Have a conversation

One senior manager told me recently that when he saw his team sending emails to one another from across the floor, he would tell them to get off their backsides and have a conversation. It infuriated him that they would sit 3 metres apart yet still send each other emails.

It is important to avoid being a constant interruption, but sometimes a conversation moves work forward more quickly and efficiently. A two-minute conversation between two people could replace 15 emails between five people. Conversations, whether face-to-face, by phone or using instant messaging (IM), are most effective when you seek *cut-through*.

Call a meeting

Meetings have a bad reputation in the productivity world, as they can be a very large waster of collective time, as discussed in chapter 5.

But they are a necessary way of getting work done. Meetings should be used sparingly, and of course should be effectively planned and run. Used well, they are a great way to move work forward, especially when we need to *collaborate*.

The conversations we have in meetings help us to make decisions, work out strategies and plans, allocate actions and brainstorm ideas.

It may be more effective to have all the relevant people in the same space at the same time in these situations.

Send an email

Email has proven to be one of the most successful communication tools ever conceived. I remember when I first used email in my role, and the joy of sending messages effortlessly, and actually getting replies!

The problem, as we have discussed, is that the volumes are now so high that managing email has become a part-time job. But email is still useful, if we can just be more thoughtful about when and how we use it.

Email is best used when *content* is most important. Delivering attached documents, or outlining our understanding of an issue can sometimes be better done in a written email, especially when it is content that the receiver can consume in their own time, rather than the minute it is sent.

Share a post

A post is a comment on a shared platform such as Slack, Yammer, Enterprise Facebook or a CRM (Customer Relationship Manager).

This communication method is becoming more and more popular in modern workplaces, but there is often confusion about how it should be used.

These tools are effective when readers need *context*. They will see a thread of the conversations within the context of the project, the topic, the issue or, in the case of a CRM tool, the client.

There is no absolute rule about when you should use one tool over another to communicate.

You and your team should start to think about when it might be good to choose certain tools over others when communicating.

Do we really need a meeting for that, or could we just have a quick phone conversation? Could we agree to post these conversations on Slack so people can read them when they have time instead of being hit by 20 emails?

All it takes is some thought and discussion.

A challenge to all managers

I am originally from Dublin. One thing I have to say for the Irish is that when we get behind something, we really get behind it. We were one of the first countries to ban smoking in public places. That was an amazing achievement, given the high rates of smoking when I was a kid. Then we banned the plastic bag in supermarkets. I remember going back on a holiday and getting filthy looks from people when I did not have a reusable bag with me when shopping. I'm sorry, I didn't know!

To change the behaviours of a nation so quickly requires clear objectives, strong leadership and an inspiring reason for people to follow and make the effort.

Changing the email culture in your team is just the same. Wouldn't it be wonderful to create a work environment where we were not drowning under a daily flood of emails? Given

---

the alternative options we have available to collaborate and communicate, this should be possible.

Imagine if we could reduce the average volume of daily email to a more manageable level for everyone in our team. What effect would that have on productivity? What if we returned to the email volumes of ten years ago? What would that be like? How much more would we get done if we could get back to a simpler world?

So why not make this your project for the next quarter? Would that not be a truly impactful contribution you could make as a manager or a leader?

EXPERT INTERVIEW
Harley Alexander — on alternatives to email

Many of us work in a world in which email is the primary mode of communication, and we probably can't imagine any other way. But there is a whole new generation who work in a different way and can't imagine using email as their main communication tool. They use a range of other tools, many of them taking their cues from social platforms such as Facebook and Snapchat.

To get my head around all this, I spoke to Harley Alexander, a web designer and 'digital problem solver'. Harley is a part of a young breed of tech-savvy entrepreneurs who think and communicate differently.

I first asked him about the proposed 'death of email'.

The main tool he and his team currently use is Slack, a seriously popular cloud-based team communication tool.

At the moment, and probably for the next five years or so, email will still be quite ubiquitous. I definitely feel the older generations hang on to it quite a lot, and it's the best tool for them to use to communicate, but it's not necessarily the most effective tool.

It's really good for high-level negotiations and large parcels of information, but when it's more transactional, like giving feedback, that's when I think it really starts to fall apart. The other thing that falls apart is really long threads of communication, just because everyone has a signature, which sometimes doubles and triples the length of every email and makes it really hard to scan.

So Harley and his team use email when they have to communicate with external parties, and when that is the preference of the client, but internally they use tools such as Slack.

A clue to the value of Slack is probably buried in its name. Apparently, Slack is an acronym for Searchable Log of All Conversation and Knowledge. I asked him how Slack helps his team to communicate efficiently.

Slack, I think, is really the opposite of email. It is great for less formal interactions, like asking quick questions, shooting the breeze about an idea. But it also brings a highly searchable way of looking through your communications and feedback and discussions, and it can act like a feed of activity.

Harley reckons that tools such as Slack offer a lot more 'context' than email. They tend to organise conversations around a topic, issue or project. Rather than having conversations buried in everyone's inboxes, they are centrally organised in a conversation thread. Users can quickly scroll through a conversation and see everyone's comments, and immediately get the context.

But this access to a stream of conversations can come at a price. Firstly, Slack and similar tools tend to be a lot more reactive. In my experience, users tend to be more prone to interruption and distraction, because they are constantly watching these feeds, or are frequently interrupted with quick questions.

They can also be subject to overwhelm, as they end up seeing every comment from every person, rather than seeing only the communications that are sent to them specifically. Tools such as Slack allow users to message one another privately, but in many ways this negates the value of the contextual feed. Harley does not always see this as a bad thing.

> *I think during a project, even if the marketing person is watching the developers talk, it's still good. Unless it's highly technical, it's still good to sort of have a bird's eye view of what everyone's doing in every department.*
>
> *You can set up sub-channels, so you have one channel for development and one channel for marketing, for example, and you can still access all that information if you need to, but you don't get pinged about it and distracted by it every five minutes.*
>
> *On a super-large project, you might have several channels, but if it's a project that runs for only four to eight weeks you can probably get away with having just one channel. The notification preferences can be set so you only get pinged when someone mentions your name. That can be quite handy in filtering out all the noise. Then when someone needs you they can @ someone and that sends the notification.*
>
> *So there are ways to filter the amount of noise that Slack makes and how much information you need to receive, but I definitely think it's good that everyone in a project can get a picture of everything.*

This is a very different proposition from email, which I see as a 'push' technology. We push information and communications into other people's inboxes. A communication tool such as Slack, on the other hand, is a 'pull' technology. We post the information, and 'pull' the relevant people to it, potentially providing much more context, and making it quicker and easier for people to 'scan' and get the gist of what is happening.

I believe email still has a role in today's workplace, especially when sending documents or requesting action, but maybe we should open our minds to using tools such as Slack, Yammer, Enterprise Facebook or whatever other cloud-based communication solution is being adopted in our team.

I asked Harley for his top three tips for people who want to expand their thinking and use tools such as Slack to complement email.

There's a fine balance between overusing collaboration tools and underusing them, but I think you need to figure out what works for you and really commit to those tools. Secondly, it's important to get everyone on board and understand how they work, otherwise communication can really start to break down.

My third tip is to avoid meetings if you can, because they soak up time and remove people from the meaningful work they should be focusing on. Meetings can be almost completely replaced by using collaboration tools effectively. We've got one client at the moment who just loves having meetings to discuss feedback that they've already left via the collaboration tools. We just find that a huge waste of time for everyone involved.

So reports of the death of email are greatly exaggerated. But we do have some new kids on the block, and they are getting massive traction in certain industries for a reason. We need to get ahead of the curve and learn to reduce the noise in our inboxes now, before we drown. Slack and similar tools may be a part of the solution.

A more thoughtful approach to communications

Asking the right questions is the key to sending focused and clear communications.

The 'W questions' we discussed at the opening of this section provide a simple structure that we can use whenever we send an email or make a post on any type of communication platform.

Figure 4.2 looks at a three-step process for writing a communication using *why*, *what* and *who*:

1. **Plan the WHY.** Every communication deserves some time spent on planning. This may range from in-depth planning for a critical report to a few moments spent focusing your

thoughts before responding to an email. The key to planning is to get clear about what outcome you want to achieve with your communication. And double-check that you are using the best communication tool for the job!

2. **Write the WHAT.** Next, you need to write the communication. But if you want the recipient to take notice and act on your communication appropriately, you need to write it in a structured way and make it easy to access. The key to writing an effective communication is to make it easy for the reader to understand and respond.

3. **Send to WHO.** Lastly, you need to consider who needs to know. If using email, who should be in the 'To' field and who should be in the CC field? If it is a response to a group email, should you Reply All or not? (I suggest probably not.) Should you send the communication to a few specific people or to a group list?

Figure 4.2: questions to ask when communicating

Planning effective communications (why)

The key thing you need to consider when planning a communication is what outcome you want to achieve. Do you need someone to *do* something? Do you simply need a timely *response*? Do you need a *decision* made? Are you just providing information to one or a number of people?

The communication method you use, and how you construct the communication, will influence the result you get.

Put yourself in your reader's shoes

By thinking about the reader, their workstyle, their role and the pressures they face, you can get a better feeling for the best way to communicate and achieve cut-through. If you are emailing your boss's boss, and you know they are in meetings most of the day, you might consider sending a short, high-impact email with a subject line that grabs their attention.

If you are communicating with a stakeholder in a project who does not know you very well, you may need to build rapport early in the communication by mentioning a common connection you both have worked with.

If you are delegating actions to multiple members of your team, you might consider outlining the actions, and who is responsible for what, upfront in the email.

You may decide that email is not the best way to communicate with someone. Considering their communication preferences, you may conclude that you will have a better chance of connecting through a channel such as Yammer or Slack, if it is used in your organisation.

Each of these strategies achieves a specific outcome. You need to take the time to plan the communication, and think about the outcome and the reader.

If you consider the productivity qualities you are aspiring to operate by as a smart team player, this approach will tick at least two of the four boxes. You are being *purposeful* by thinking about the outcome you want to achieve, and you are being *mindful* by putting yourself in the reader's shoes.

Manage your communication brand

One of my senior clients came to me for help with her email. When I asked her what drove her to reach out for the coaching, she shared with me that she felt that her brand was being damaged by her use of email.

While she was an extremely competent leader and executive, her inbox was out of control. She kept missing important emails and was behind on a lot of actions. But it was not just her management of incoming email that damaged her brand. Her outgoing emails did not look good either. She was generally rushing from one meeting to another, trying to stay on top of the deluge, reacting on the run. This led to poorly written emails, unclear communications and frequent misunderstandings.

As a senior female leader in a large organisation, she knew that these things created an impression, and could damage her brand as a top-level executive.

Luckily, she had the common sense to do something about it.

How about you?

Writing effective communications (what)

A friend of mine once worked in the attorney-general's office. When she or any of the team had to meet with the director-general, they were expected to prepare a 20-minute overview of the issue, as well as a two-minute summary. They knew that, as his schedule shifted, their meeting could be pared down to two minutes, and they were expected to be able to succinctly nail the issue and any recommendations in two minutes. This was very hard to do, but it taught her a great skill.

Think about what you are trying to achieve with your email, and the best way to make it easy for the reader to get your point quickly.

Your reader is usually busy, distracted, bored, on the run or overwhelmed. Or all of the above. If you want to get cut-through in a world where 100-plus messages a day is normal, you need to stand out by writing well-structured and concise communications that help the reader to understand the issue, question, request or recommendation quickly.

It will benefit the reader because they don't have to do as much work to understand what is needed. It will benefit you as they are more likely to action the email in a timely way. Win–win.

This is another example of game theory productivity, discussed in chapter 2. It is about working with others in a way that is productive for you, as well as being productive for the group.

Mark Twain once apologised in a letter to his brother for writing such a long letter, explaining that he did not have time to write a short one. Writing brief but instructive emails takes more time, which may be less 'efficient' but is a lot more effective.

Your emails need to be read, be actioned and create flow rather than friction.

Make it easy for the reader

Qualities: *Purposeful, Mindful*

Do yourself and the recipients a favour by writing emails in a way that makes it easy for them to understand your message. This is a win–win. They find it easier to engage with your email. You will have your email actioned more quickly.

The three ingredients of good communication

Think about an email you received recently that made you instantly recoil and think, 'I can't even look at this right now.' What was it about the email that made you roll your cursor over it and move on to the next one? I would guess it was missing three essential ingredients that make you want to open it, or at least feel able to open it, there and then.

The first ingredient is *focus*. We need communications to quickly focus our attention on the issue, the request or the relevant information. *What is this about?*

The second ingredient is *clarity*. When you are not clear in your communication to me, it causes friction for me. I then need to seek clarification from you, in turn causing you friction. This results in wasted time and frustration for both of us, because not enough care was taken with the initial communication.

The third and final ingredient is *context*. Readers need context to understand how this fits into the bigger picture, and they may need additional supporting information to find that context. The key is to give them the context in a way that is quick to access if they choose to.

Don't waste their time by forcing them to read three paragraphs of background before you get to the point.

Make the headlines

One strategy that can help your emails achieve cut-through, and get actioned, is to write a strong subject line. In an article in the *Harvard Business Review*, Kabir Sehgal talks about the success the US military had with changing how emails were written in the field. For them, a clear or unclear communication could be a matter of life or death.

He outlined a set of keywords that were often used at the start of a subject line to clearly communicate upfront what was required:

ACTION. The recipient is required to take action.

SIGN. The recipient's signature is required.

INFO. No action is needed (for information only).

(continued)

Make the headlines (*cont'd*)

DECISION. The recipient is required to make and communicate a decision.

REQUEST. The sender seeks the recipient's agreement or approval.

COORD. Coordination is needed between sender and recipient.

It is well worth compiling your own set of keywords that are relevant to your team.

The SSS approach to emails

A simple format for writing effective emails is to slow down and use the SSS approach (see figure 4.3):

1. **Subject**. Write a clear subject line that accurately describes the contents. We are often lazy with subject lines, and don't bother changing old ones. Think of the subject line as comparable to a newspaper headline. It needs to be accurate and to grab the reader's attention. A strong subject line creates *focus*.

Figure 4.3: the SSS approach to emails

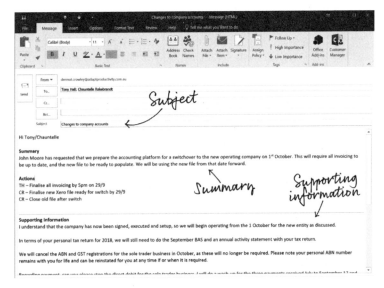

2. **Summary**. Start the email with a short 'executive summary' so the reader can understand the context and any recommendations at a glance. This should also include a list of actions required from the email. By putting these upfront you will find that more people will read and action your email in a timely way. A clear summary provides *clarity*.

3. **Supporting information**. Finally, write or attach the supporting information so that the reader can delve into this if and when necessary. Appropriate supporting information provides *context*.

A strong subject line creates FOCUS.

A clear summary provides CLARITY.

Appropriate supporting information provides CONTEXT.

Top 12 email writing tips

Here are some more ideas that will help you to write emails that make communication easier for you as well as the reader.

1. Keep the email short and to the point. Brevity is not rude.

2. Write a relevant subject line that describes the purpose of the email.

3. Summarise the issue, question or recommendation in the first paragraph (see the SSS approach).

4. List any actions required near the top of the email.

5. Where possible, frame the email to require a simple Yes or No response.

6. If you require a more complex response, give the reader an A, B or C choice.

7. Outline what you expect to happen in different scenarios.

8. Format the email using headers, paragraphs and bullet points to help the reader digest the information.

9. Use subject codes such as ACT or FYI to communicate what is required in the subject line.

(*continued*)

Top 12 email writing tips (*cont'd*)

10. Review what you have written before you send it, and tighten it up even more.

11. Spellcheck every email.

12. Don't expect actions from people you have copied by CC.

Sending effective communications (who)

Before pressing Send, have a final think about who needs to know. We create so much noise, especially with the overuse of email, and we have a responsibility to reduce that noise as much as possible while still doing what we need to do to fulfil our role.

One of my clients, new to a role in a tech company, complained of the flood of emails in his inbox, a conversation that had been raging there for a couple of weeks. He counted more than 60 emails in the thread, yet the conversation was not central to him, his team or his boss!

Email noise is a shared problem, and it needs a shared solution. To have any chance of staying on top of our priorities, we need to reduce this noise, as I discussed in my first book, *Smart Work*. There I reviewed strategies for reducing the noise, ranging from getting off distribution and CC lists to setting automated rules to redirect or delete emails.

I talked about the three main categories of email that we receive:

- action emails
- informational emails
- junk emails.

Only some of these emails are useful to us and are needed in our role, but many are just *noise*. *Smart Work* looked at ways to reduce this noise. Now we need to look at the other side of this issue, and examine how we can minimise the noise we ourselves create.

Think about the noise you potentially generate for your team and colleagues.

Noise can be created by:

- CC emails that do not add value for the recipient
- nonessential Reply All conversations in which the recipient is an observer rather than a participant
- thank you emails (most of the time)
- emails sent to a general distribution list rather than a more targeted group
- system-generated emails that duplicate other workflows
- nonessential chatter and discussion.

Of course, all of the above examples are relevant sometimes, but most of the time they just hamper us from getting to the important stuff.

Pause, think, send

As a kid learning to cross the road, you may have been taught some variant of the caution 'Stop, Look, Cross'. This slogan was designed to help young children recall the main steps involved in crossing the road safely, but it also served as a circuit-breaker, to get your mind out of 'auto mode' and get you fully engaged with what you were doing.

A good way to short-circuit our automatic habits around email is to develop a similar mantra around sending email: 'Pause, Think, Send'. Getting into the habit of mentally rehearsing these three words before you press Send can pull you out of 'auto-mode', reminding you to check that you have written the email well, addressed it to the right people, attached the relevant document, and so on.

Try it and see.

Noise reduction strategies

So what can we do to reduce the noise for our team and our colleagues? There are lots of simple strategies that can help, and many of them just come down to a more thoughtful approach to using email. A little more empathy for your colleagues will go a long way!

Reply with care

One wonderful advantage of email is that it allows us to communicate with one individual or a large group with equal ease—for the sender. But if we address the email to people who do not really need to know, we start to erode the tool's utility for the recipients.

If we are the original generator of the email, we are less likely to address it to too many people, as it takes effort to include them all in the address field. But when we receive an email that has been sent to a group, we need only click the Reply All button to send our response to the whole group.

It is too easy for us to absent-mindedly Reply All to email after email, often filling other people's inboxes with messages that are not relevant to them.

Imagine the support person in your team sends out an email to the entire team asking about dietary requirements or special preferences for catering for the team offsite next week. In such a case those with special requirements should reply directly, and *only*, *to* the sender. But how often does the whole group receive gratuitous Reply All responses informing them of Anna's allergy to shellfish or Peter's dislike of mushrooms!

We could reduce the number of times this situation arises in two ways. First, the team assistant could indicate clearly that any responses should be directed to her and her only. This would require a one-sentence instruction at the start of the email:

Please respond with your preferences only to me.

or

Please direct any questions to Matt and Carol.

This instruction would help the rest of the team enormously, as it would give them clear direction and remind them of the appropriate action to take.

A second solution is for you, as the recipient of the email, to take a moment before replying to think about who really needs to receive your response.

Reduce email noise

Qualities: *Purposeful, Mindful*

Try not to add to the cacophony of noise created every day in your workplace. Be purposeful in your communications, and take some of the load off your teammates' inboxes.

Don't be a copy cat

CC (for 'carbon copy') is a holdover from the good old days when paper memos were delivered by hand to managers and executives. If other people needed to be looped in on the memo, carbon paper was used to create duplicate copies.

In the days of paper memos this was used judiciously as you could only put a certain amount of pressure on the page when writing, so the number of copies was very limited. And people thought carefully about who needed to know, and why.

But with email, the CC field is all too easy to populate, so we do. And it is easier still to CC a whole team distribution list. Extra points for that, I reckon!

While there is value in keeping your team in the loop, there is also a cost if this opportunity is not used judiciously or for the right reasons.

My clients tell me that much of the time they are copied in for the benefit of the sender rather than the recipients. We are CC'd for political reasons, as part of a power game. We are copied in because the sender wants to show how busy they are, or because the sender is obsessed about keeping everyone in every loop, just in case. Information is power, until we can't digest it effectively—then it is just noise.

The solution to this problem is similar as for the Reply All issue.

Think carefully before copying people in. Do they really need to know this? Why?

It is also useful to discuss with your team what you do and don't need or expect to be copied in on. This could take the form of a general discussion about your preferences, or relate to a specific project or issue. Giving people clear direction in this way saves time for you and them.

As the recipient of CC emails, you might also take steps to reduce the noise that you receive. In *Smart Work*, I talked about the idea of setting up a CC folder, and having all CC's directed automatically to this folder when they arrive. This means you have created a second, lower priority inbox that can be checked periodically, when you have time. If you do this, it is critical that you discuss it with your team, your peers and key stakeholders, so they are aware of your method.

It is important that everyone in your team knows never to put actions for recipients who are listed in the CC field. No one should miss an action because they assumed the email was sent merely to keep them in the loop.

To copy or not to copy

I had to make a CC decision just the other day. I was sending an email to Chris, the managing editor at Wiley to give him a progress update on a manuscript deadline. My initial point of contact at Wiley was Lucy, the senior commissioning editor. It was a significant deadline, but all was on track.

I considered copying Lucy, as I felt that she would appreciate the peace of mind, knowing the manuscript was on track. Then I remembered her handover email to Chris and myself, and I recalled that she had clearly stated that there was no need to copy her in on the day-to-day stuff.

So I did not copy her in, figuring that Chris would keep her in the loop on progress. One less email for Lucy. I hope she appreciates me!

CC with purpose

Qualities: *Purposeful, Mindful*

Copying others in on an email has value in certain situations. Use this function carefully and thoughtfully, though. Consider first why you are copying them, and whether they really need this communication.

Use distribution lists carefully

I work in many organisations where group distribution lists are still used as a very blunt communication tool. Emails will be sent to whole teams, departments and sometimes divisions using these lists. All too often, the content of the message is relevant to a sub-group but largely irrelevant to all others. The problem is that it is much easier to send to the full list than to select only the individuals who need to know.

I do see this happening less in organisations that have embraced other communication platforms such as Enterprise Facebook, Slack or Yammer, but the problem still exists.

One strategy that can help here is to take the time to create more segmented lists at the team level, so a communication can be sent to a team or several teams without too much work being involved. And of course, the lists should be kept up to date if they are to serve. Surely having one person spend time on the upkeep of these lists is a better use of resources than everyone having to deal with extraneous noise?

Another strategy is to move to another platform for this type of communication. If it is a broad announcement, or information that should be made available to the group, maybe posting it on an enterprise social media platform would be more efficient and relevant.

Email lists should be used only by a few, and only occasionally, to keep noise levels low and ensure the right information gets to the right people only.

Get up and talk to someone

This is a really simple but important point. Stop typing that email to the person sitting opposite you. Get up, go over and talk to them. You might like them!

More than three emails—have a chat

Qualities: *Purposeful, Mindful*

Reduce the email load on your colleagues by nipping email conversations in the bud. When you spot an email conversation developing, pick up the phone or find the key people involved and have a chat.

Thanks, but no thanks

You do not always need to say thanks in response to an email. Do I really need to tell you this? Unfortunately, yes. I have had this conversation with clients for years, yet the topic never goes away.

I get that we want to be polite and friendly to our colleagues and clients, but in doing so we are causing them more noise and more work. So think before you respond to an email simply to say thanks. Think hard. Is it really necessary?

Most of the time it won't be. And believe me, 99 per cent of the time you will not offend the sender. I would love to measure the loss of productivity in the corporate workplace caused by well-intentioned 'thank you' noise. I suggest we all say thank you to each other during our Monday meeting for all of the things we will send each other in the coming week. Then it is done, and we can all enjoy less email overload.

Of course sometimes 'thank you' is useful, as well as courteous—for example:

- when someone has gone out of their way to deliver something, and you want to show true appreciation

- when the information received is critical in some way, and your acknowledgement will give the sender peace of mind

- when the relationship needs reinforcement or a bit of TLC

- when the sender has requested it.

EXPERT INTERVIEW
Paul Jones—on effective email writing

How much friction do you suppose we cause our colleagues simply because we do not take the time to write effective emails? A lot, I reckon.

I talked to expert business writer Paul Jones about this. Paul has many years' experience working as a copywriter and a business writing coach and trainer, and has some useful thinking on how we can make our communications easier to read. I asked Paul what distinguishes a well-written email from a poorly written one.

For me, the quality of communication comes down to one thing: did you achieve your goal? What was your goal? Maybe it was to inform someone of something, and make sure they understood it. Maybe it was to persuade or to build a relationship, or even to entertain.

This echoes points that I have made earlier in this section. Start with the end in mind, start with *why*. Paul recommends we first take some time to think about what we want to achieve. He then suggests we make our communications easy for the recipient to read.

Clear subject headers, get to the point, be brief, and if that means using a graphic, even in emails, you can do that these days. Headers, subheaders and bullets. And make it as skimmable as possible.

Brevity is a key consideration, Paul believes. We often feel the need to write lots of content to fully explain an issue, but most readers don't have time to read pages and pages of background. They want to get to the heart of the issue quickly, and then delve into the supporting information if and when they need to.

> *I was running a course for one of the big four banks. I checked in with the manager who booked it to ask, 'Is there anything I should know about the people coming?'*
>
> *He said, 'Actually, yes. There's one person I should mention. She's got a PhD in maths, super bright, but no one likes reading her emails.' I asked, 'Why not?' He said, 'Because you'll ask her the simplest question and get back this great, long, overly detailed email response. It just takes so much time to read and figure out the core of the message. It's actually affected her productivity, because now people will read her emails last instead of first.'*

It can take more time to write a concise, brief email, but it saves time in the long run for everyone involved. And it increases the chance that others will read and action your communications.

On ways to get more cut-through when sending emails, Paul suggests knowing your audience is key. It helps to have some understanding of them and their role, and some empathy for the pressures they are under.

> *Treat every reader as if they're lazy, busy and selfish. If you don't treat them as lazy, busy and selfish, you are more likely to make it about you, and not them. You won't write it with their needs in mind. It also means you won't be respecting their time.*

Before sending an email, Paul suggests, think hard about whether you should even send it. Is there a better way to communicate what you need to? Would the receiver be more open to a phone call, or a face-to-face discussion, or even a text message? Keep the reader in mind always.

Finally, Paul emphasises the importance of making sure your emails are well written, and spelt and punctuated correctly.

Punctuation is like road signs. If you put the punctuation in the wrong place, or don't use it where you should, or it is used incorrectly, people may get the wrong idea and misunderstand your message. It can also give the impression that you are uneducated.

Many people are overconfident and have big blind spots with their communications. It is important to recognise that before we send out anything we have written, we need to look it over again with fresh eyes. We are bound to have missed something, or made an embarrassing error or expressed something unclearly, or missed an essential point we should have included.

None of this is terribly hard or complicated. Our important communications simply require some thought and effort, and the investment of a little time.

Okay, by adopting some of the strategies discussed in this chapter, we should have reduced the noise we are creating for our colleagues, and the noise we ourselves are subject to. Now to that other huge drain on our time — meetings.

5

CONGREGATE: MAKE MEETINGS COUNT

Meetings are a common way in which we cooperate together—but, oh boy, do they take up our time! Many of my senior clients spend most of their week in meetings, while middle managers and other staff can spend as much as two days a week in these sessions. This can be a huge drain on productivity, especially if the meetings are not well organised.

The sad fact is that too many of our meetings are unnecessary, take too much time and are poorly planned.

If we want to create a culture that supports productivity, we need to have fewer meetings. I don't imagine that any reader would disagree with this, especially at a senior level, where meetings can take up to 90 per cent of an executive's day.

What's wrong with our meeting culture?

The three key problems with our dysfunctional meeting culture are:

1. too much time spent in meetings

2. too many 'fuzzy' meetings that are poorly planned with no clearly stated outcomes

3. poor meeting behaviours that cause productivity friction.

1. Too much time in meetings

In a coaching session with a senior client last year, we sat in front of his calendar to find a good time to plan a critical new project. I knew we would be hard pressed to find any available time over the coming couple of weeks. But as we scrolled through week after week of back-to-back meetings, double-booked meetings, all-day meetings and recurring meetings, I realised just how bad this problem was.

He needed to flip forward eight weeks before he could find a three-hour timeslot to schedule the project planning session. This executive is not alone. His situation is extreme, certainly, but is becoming more and more the norm. Our days are being taken over by endless meetings.

If we spend too much of our time trapped in meetings our balance goes out of whack. Senior executives still have other priorities, things they must get done outside of meetings, but they leave themselves no time to do them. They are stuck in meetings from 9 am to 5 pm, then spend from 5 pm to 9 pm catching up on their other work and checking emails. Under such pressure, the quality of their work suffers.

While this problem may not be so extreme at more junior levels, many of us spend a lot of our time in meetings, and too much of that time is used less than effectively. There is no balance in the schedule, which leads to long working hours, increased stress and growing frustration.

2. Poorly planned and poorly run meetings

One of the negative impacts of being so busy is we don't have the time or the headspace to properly plan the meetings we organise or attend. This leads to wasted time in the meeting and the risk that it will not achieve a clear outcome.

Many of us plan the meeting in the meeting. We turn up and say, 'Okay, what are we here to talk about?'

Of course, many meetings — especially the more formal ones — are planned well, with all participants ensuring they are prepared. But less formal and structured meetings without a clear purpose or agenda are at greater risk of meandering unproductively.

3. Poor meeting behaviours

One day, as I was waiting for a workshop to start in one of my professional services client firms, the HR manager who organised the training gave me a heads up that some people were likely to arrive late.

She explained that they operated at a different 'pace' to most organisations, and that people often arrived a few minutes late to internal meetings. I braced myself for a couple of latecomers. The reality was much worse than I had anticipated.

Out of 19 participants, just two arrived on time. The rest dribbled in over a period of 15 minutes after the session was to have started. Not one person apologised for being late. This way of operating had been normalised for them, and they did not see it as a problem. It was shocking to me, and spoke volumes about the culture of the organisation. I was sure that if I followed the senior leadership team around for a week, I would see them displaying the same disrespect for other people's time.

When I discussed this at the break with the HR person, she admitted it was a big problem, but she assured me it would never happen at client meetings — only internal ones. So it seems that they were happy to respect time when there was a sale on the line, but not if it was just for the benefit of the team. This suggests that they set no value on their colleagues' time. And the behaviour was perpetuated because there were no consequences.

This was such a good example of poor meeting behaviour that had become normalised across the team. The culture of an organisation is shaped by behaviour like this.

But it is not the only poor meeting behaviour. Spot the behaviours that are common in your workplace among the following:

- stepping in and out of the room to take calls during the meeting
- doing emails instead of being attentive
- staying quiet in the meeting, but raising issues afterwards
- dominating the discussion unreasonably
- dismissing the points of view of others
- having side conversations when someone is talking
- hijacking the agenda.

Which poor meeting behaviours are you guilty of?

So how can you ensure that your meetings play a productive part in how you and your team get work done?

Let's aim for 100 per cent fewer meetings

I am a bit tired of working in organisations where many managers and leaders spend most of their day in back-to-back meetings. It is not necessary, and it is not productive. Imagine if we had 100 per cent fewer meetings in our organisations.

That's right, 100 per cent. How could this be? How could we get anything meaningful done without coming together in meetings, at least occasionally?

Okay, I don't really want to eradicate meetings altogether, but I would like to see four 25 per cent decreases when it comes to our meetings. Here is what I mean.

What if your team worked to reduce the *number* of meetings it held by 25 per cent over a month? Imagine you then looked at reducing the average *length* of meetings by 25 per cent. You also worked on reducing the *number of participants* in each meeting by 25 per cent. Finally, you put strategies in place to reduce *time wasted* in meetings by 25 per cent. That equals a 100 per cent reduction in meetings ... kind of. Of course, this is a bit tongue in cheek. But I put it this way to grab your attention, which is what you need to do with your team if you are to change their behaviours!

Can you see the productivity uplift if we tightened up in these areas? It would be massive! And, I believe, not that hard to achieve.

25 per cent fewer meetings

There is a lot of fat in the meeting system. The number of meetings we commit to could be pared back. It would take a conscious effort though, and the erection of some boundaries around how time is used in our week.

Rather than seeing our schedule as a 'free for all', where any available timeslot could be seized on as an opportunity to meet, we should aim for a balance in our week. This would depend on our role, of course.

In most roles no more than half of our work hours should be allocated for meetings. This means half of the time is protected to get other stuff done.

This is a game we can play with ourselves. If we decide that half of our week should be protected from meetings, then we need to get creative on how we meet the demands of the business and protect our boundaries.

The first step is to attend meetings only if they have a clear purpose and value. (More on this later.) A second step is to look for creative ways to achieve an objective without a meeting, for example through a quick conversation, a phone call, or a written brief or report.

Finally, we should see our available time as a resource we need to manage carefully. We cannot fill our jug to the brim and not expect some spillage. We need a mark that says 'Do not fill beyond this point'. That should be our 'high meeting level', to be exceeded only in extreme circumstances.

Again, I am not denying that meetings can be a critical tool for progressing work. We do not need to eliminate meetings altogether. I am suggesting a meeting diet. Let's cut the fat.

Here are some strategies to help reduce the number of meetings:

- Don't just default to a meeting—consider the alternatives.
- Clarify the meeting's purpose—you might find it is not needed in this case.
- Review all regular team meetings. Are they necessary?
- Downgrade a meeting to a conversation.

> **Count every meeting—make every meeting count**
>
>
> **Qualities:** *Purposeful, Mindful*
>
> Call a meeting only if it is necessary. Ensure you are not meeting simply because it is what you have always done or it seems the easiest option. Imagine you had to justify the cost of every meeting in the same way you do your travel expenses!

25 per cent shorter meeting durations

Why are most meetings scheduled for an hour? Is it because the total time needed to cover the agenda items equals an hour? I don't think so. It is because most calendars divide your day into one-hour timeslots, and this has become the default.

In a humorous essay in *The Economist* in 1955, C. Northcote Parkinson proposed what has become known as Parkinson's Law, which states that 'work expands so as to fill the time available for its completion'.

If you schedule a meeting for an hour, it will take one hour. If you schedule it for 45 minutes (a 25 per cent reduction in duration), it will take 45 minutes, and you may even get more work done, as everyone will be more focused.

Again, there is a lot of fat in the system here. We all tend to fall into default thinking patterns and go with accepted norms or patterns.

If over the next month you were to challenge yourself to reduce the time allotted to every meeting you schedule, you might be pleasantly surprised. And this goes for the meeting invitations you accept as well.

Challenge whether you really need an hour for a meeting, and you may find many meetings can be completed more quickly.

This may also have a flow-on effect, as colleagues and teammates begin to change their default thinking and propose shorter meetings.

Please don't take this to mean that all one-hour meetings should be replaced by 45-minute meetings. *Meeting durations should suit the content and agenda.* Why have a 45-minute meeting when we only need 15 minutes?

The idea that the agenda should dictate the duration of the meeting is critical to productivity in a collaborative workplace, and will be explored in more detail later.

Here are some strategies to reduce the length of meetings:

- Plan the agenda and set the meeting length as needed.
- Agree in your team on 25- or 45-minute meeting time defaults.
- Leave small talk until the end of the meeting.
- Focus the meeting at the start, and clearly define the proposed outcomes.
- Meet by phone or online if these are options.
- Ensure there is a clock in the room so everyone can monitor the time.

Wrap it up early

Qualities: *Purposeful, Reliable*

Make sure that everyone gets out the door on time by starting to wrap up the meeting when there are still five or ten minutes to go. Check to see if any agenda items need to be dealt with offline, and that everyone has committed to their actions.

25 per cent fewer participants

I once ran a session with a senior technical team in one of the big banks in Australia. They complained about how most of their days were spent in meetings, and they often ended up triple-booked as senior stakeholders in the wider bank made heavy demands on their time.

They described many meetings that would include up to a dozen participants, with only one or two people actually talking throughout the meeting. Really? A dozen spectators? Do that many people need to be present to listen to one or two technical experts? Could the decisions/ideas/strategies discussed in that meeting be communicated to the wider group in a more efficient way? Absolutely!

We fall into the trap of inviting everyone to cover all bases,
but this reduces the productivity of many, if not most,
of the people involved.

Research suggests that including any more than seven participants in a meeting makes decision making harder. In fact, a study by Bain & Company found that every attendee over seven reduced the decision effectiveness by 10 per cent. In larger groups, everyone may have an opinion, which can complicate clear decision making. With larger groups side conversations can erupt, which takes authority away from the meeting leader. Larger groups (if well facilitated) may work well when the meeting purpose is to brainstorm or generate ideas, but often less is more.

Jeff Bezos, CEO of Amazon, relies on his 'two pizza rule': Meeting participants should not exceed the number that could be fed comfortably by two pizzas. That gives a little bit of wiggle room when you consider how a pizza could be carved up, but you get the idea. The two-pizza analogy helps us keep in mind the importance of holding the numbers down when organising meetings.

Here are a few other strategies to reduce the number of participants in meetings:

- List the participants and their reason for attending.
- Create an agenda and invite people based on this.
- Use the 'Required' field only for people who must attend.
- Use the 'Optional' field for those participants who are not essential, but who you feel should have the option to attend if they wish.

> ### Check availability when scheduling meetings
>
> **Qualities:** *Purposeful, Mindful*
>
> Don't send meeting invites without checking participants' availability in the scheduling system. If unsure, pick up the phone and check if they are available. Don't just blindly hope for the best.

25 per cent less time wasted

Finally, what can we do to increase the quality of our meetings, and to decrease wasted time, focus and energy? Well-planned meetings with a clearly stated purpose that are attended by the right people and are driven by a strong agenda will get the most out of the allocated time for all involved.

Do you believe that most of your meetings fit this description? Or are they a little fuzzy? Fuzzy meetings often start a bit late, have no clear direction or agenda, and finish as participants of the next meeting are knocking on the door. They also probably end without any clear actions or decisions, which may require a further meeting to establish.

To ensure it is focused, not fuzzy, we need to bring to the meeting an agreed process.

To ensure a productive outcome, there are things we need to do *before* the meeting, *during* the meeting and *after* the meeting. Later in this chapter we will explore strategies for planning and organising an effective meeting. For the moment, however, consider if the following strategies might help to reduce wasted time in your meetings:

- Plan the meeting beforehand, including establishing the meeting purpose and agenda.

- Send the agenda to participants well ahead of the meeting.

- Distil supporting information to make it easy for the attendees to grasp.

- Begin the meeting by focusing everyone on the agenda.

- Run the agenda to time.

- Redirect new topics to a 'parking lot' for future meetings.

- Manage personalities that may derail the meeting agenda.

- Ensure participants capture and own their actions.

- Pause and agree on the best use of the final ten minutes.

- Evaluate every meeting.

If we work as a team to apply the 100 per cent fewer meetings principle to our work, the productivity gains will be huge.

Turn up on time

Qualities: *Punctual, Mindful, Reliable*

Have enough respect for your colleagues to arrive on time to the meeting—'on time' meaning a few minutes before the scheduled start. This is not hard to do if you manage your schedule with this concept in mind.

The five-finger test

My dear friend Georgia Murch works with many Australian businesses on their feedback culture. She shares a strategy for quickly evaluating the effectiveness of a meeting that she picked up from a client.

She calls it the five-finger test.

At the end of the meeting, get all of the participants to rate the meeting by raising between one and five fingers—one finger means it was pretty poor, and five means it was excellent. Then ask the fours and fives what worked so they can keep doing that, and ask the ones and twos what reduced the meeting's effectiveness, so they can fix that.

(continued)

The five-finger test (*cont'd*)

I imagine if meeting organisers in your team adopted this little exercise consistently, it would have a hugely positive effect on your meeting culture. The thing I like about this strategy is that it is quick and painless, which takes the friction out of doing it consistently.

Make your meetings more effective

Think of a recent meeting you organised. You probably jumped into your calendar, chose a time that suited your schedule, checked if others were available and, after a bit of back and forth, sent an invite for the obligatory one-hour meeting with some vague title, assuming that everyone would know generally what was going to be discussed.

You then arrive at the meeting, possibly late, and wait for all the participants to arrive from their previous meetings, also possibly late. Most of the planning for the meeting is done in the meeting itself and, if there is an agenda, you probably don't manage to cover all the key items as you get bogged down on side issues that really are not that important anyway.

I know I paint a bleak picture, and I am being unfair to the many people who really make an effort to organise their meetings well. But I believe we will all see something of our own experience in this description.

Meetings are a luxury and use up more resources than any other type of business activity, so they should be planned well to maximise the return on investment of time and resources.

Once you have decided a meeting is necessary, you have a responsibility to ensure that it is planned and run effectively. So how do we get the most out of the time we will spend together?

Plan meetings the right way around

I think we often put the cart before the horse when organising meetings—that is, we do it the wrong way around, jumping straight into *coordinating* the logistics without first clarifying the *context* and *content*. This means we consider *who*, *where* and *when* before we consider *why* and *what*, if we reflect on these at all.

This leads to flawed thinking, and often means our meetings are fuzzy rather than focused. Think about the impact this can have on your meetings.

How can you ascertain how long the meeting should take, what type of meeting environment would be most suitable and who should be there before you have set the purpose and the agenda?

There is a better way to plan and organise a meeting so as to maximise everyone's time and attention. Let me introduce you to the 5W approach.

The 5W approach to planning meetings

As with any type of cooperative activity, we can use questions to focus our thinking and planning. Asking the 'W questions', as discussed earlier, is a great way to organise any meeting. *But only if done in the right sequence.*

It does not take that long to stop and think about these questions before you shoot off a meeting invite. And some thought about the answers will ensure the meeting is focused and organised, and involves the right people and resources. The logical flow of these questions can be overlaid on the three stages of planning a meeting, as shown in figure 5.1 (overleaf).

Figure 5.1: the 5Ws to planning a meeting

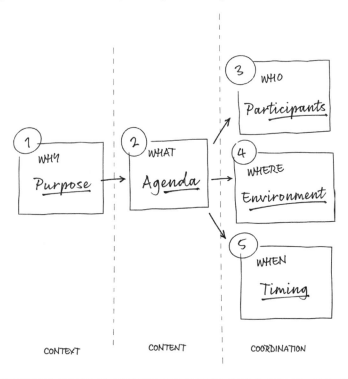

1. Why
Set the purpose

Priority number one is to clarify the meeting purpose. This sets the context and allows you to make the right decisions about when the meeting should be held, who needs to attend and how long you will need.

Setting and communicating the meeting context is probably the most important thing you can do to improve the quality of your meetings.

In his book *The 7 Habits of Highly Effective People*, Stephen Covey recommends that we start with the end in mind, which is exactly what I propose here. Everything else is driven by the meeting purpose.

While some meetings might have a mixed bag of agenda items and defined outcomes, many others will have a single focus, and the purpose of the meeting can be described in one sentence. It is essential to take a moment to really think about what you need to achieve in the meeting.

Create a *meeting purpose statement* by completing the sentence:

The purpose of this meeting is to...

This statement is not just for you, the meeting organiser. It should also be stated explicitly in the meeting invitation, preferably at the very top of the notes area so it is the first thing that recipients see after the meeting name and time.

Here are some examples of clear meeting purpose statements:

1. The purpose of this meeting is to finalise the project plan for the team offsite in June.

2. The purpose of this meeting is to decide on the invitation list for the client dinner, and to agree on the wording for the invite email.

3. The purpose of this meeting is to outline our recommendation for training needs for the coming year for the finance team.

4. The purpose of this meeting is to sign off on the marketing plan for the next financial year, and to complete the following:

   - Review and approve the budget.

   - Detail the marketing projects required.

   - Identify the external suppliers to approach for quotes.

   - Agree on resource allocation for each department.

The meeting purpose statement should use language that describes a clear deliverable or deliverables for the meeting.

While it is sometimes hard to describe a meeting's purpose in one sentence, it should help clarify for you, the organiser, why you are calling the meeting, and help the participants understand why they should be attending. As shown above, a few bullet points can identify multiple deliverables if required.

I often adopt this format for client meetings too, although in some circumstances they themselves may have called the meeting, and I am careful not to appear too pushy by organising their meeting for them. Yet they often appreciate the clarity that this can inject.

There is nothing worse than arriving at a meeting to find other participants are only vaguely aware of its purpose. Wasted time for both parties.

---

2. What
Create the agenda

Once you are clear about the meeting's purpose, you can start to work on the content. Typically, an agenda is used to communicate the content and set up a framework for discussion.

Unfortunately, many less formal meetings are held without an agenda. The agenda is more than a list of discussion points—it is an important tool to ensure a productive outcome.

An agenda should:

- clarify the thinking of the organiser
- communicate what will be covered in the meeting
- focus the thinking of the participants
- help the participants to prepare for the meeting
- allow potential participants to negotiate if they believe they are not the right person
- focus the meeting itself
- manage time in the meeting
- rank the agenda items in priority order.

Later in the chapter we will look at the different types of meeting agenda item and how they can each be managed most effectively.

Turn up fully

Qualities: *Purposeful, Mindful, Reliable*

Be present and engaged in meetings, or don't attend. Don't distract yourself or others with emails or phone calls. If the meeting is a good use of your time, then use that time for the good of the meeting.

3. Who
Choose the resources

The final elements that should be organised are the participants (who), the environment (where) and the timing (when). I believe this *coordination* can be effectively managed only once you have set the *context* and outlined the *content*.

A few years ago I was invited to attend a client meeting to provide some technical expertise on the implementation of a new communication system. The meeting, with ten participants, was poorly planned and poorly run. The external firm presenting the solution did not communicate a clear purpose to be achieved by the end of the meeting and facilitated it poorly. Everyone had an opinion but no one made a decision.

At the end of the meeting it was agreed that we would 'think about it' and organise another meeting in a few weeks. As we walked out the COO whispered to me that we had just wasted two hours of our lives. I reckoned we had just wasted 20 hours. It was obvious that the managers who attended were not the right people to make a decision and drive the project forward.

It is critical to invite the right people, and the right number of participants, to our meetings. Too few and we may miss key stakeholders. Too many and we tie up resources unnecessarily, and in some cases compromise the effectiveness of the meeting.

Different resources need to be organised for a meeting, including a room and equipment, but it is the human resources that are most important.

To achieve the best outcomes, you need the right people in the room, but no more than necessary. When planning the *who* of meetings, you need to think in terms of 'group time'. A 30-minute meeting with eight participants takes up four hours of group time. Are you prepared to waste four hours with a poorly planned meeting? Are you prepared to tie up resources in the meeting just in case they are needed?

The purpose statement and the list of agenda items and deliverables should help you determine the resources needed. Looking at each agenda item, ask yourself who is required to cover the agenda item adequately. Who is essential and who would be a discretionary choice? Remember, we are aiming for a 25 per cent reduction in meeting attendees.

It may be worth making a separate list of any stakeholders who do not need to be present at the meeting itself but who may need to be kept informed of any decisions made or outcomes achieved. Make a note to include them in any emails sent after the meeting to confirm the outcomes.

Justify the meeting invitation list

Several years ago I worked with a company who wanted to improve the effectiveness of their meetings. Their CEO was very concerned about both the number of meetings they had and the large numbers of staff who attended these meetings. He used to walk down the hallways, looking through the glass meeting-room walls and despairing at the number of staff involved in these meetings.

As we worked on a meeting agenda template to be used by his team, he asked me to add an additional element: a section in which the meeting organiser had to list the meeting participants invited, and *why* they were required.

This was a masterstroke, because it forced two behaviours. Firstly, the meeting organiser had to think hard about who was really needed and it made them more accountable. It also meant that the invitation recipients could see why they were being invited, which helped them to prepare appropriately, or gave them the opportunity to negotiate if they felt they were not the best person for the job.

4. Where
Create the right environment

I remember a client meeting where I was being briefed on a major training rollout across a whole division. The manager I was meeting with forgot to book a room, so we ended up meeting in the café area in the middle of their activity-based workplace. I needed to understand some complex issues, and this busy, noisy space was less than ideal for the purpose. We got by, but I felt the briefing could have been so much better if it had taken place in an appropriate room with access to a screen and a whiteboard.

Meetings need to be staged in a suitable environment. They are rarely productive when held in a space that does not support productivity.

The agenda will inform the environment needed. If you expect to be brainstorming, then a room with whiteboards and lots of space will work best. Obviously the room will need to accommodate the number of participants comfortably. If delegating a piece of work, you may need to plug your laptop into a screen to demonstrate or coach.

Here are some considerations when thinking about the meeting environment:

- How many participants will be attending?
- Will anyone need to link in from another location?
- Do we need electronic resources to present data via computer?
- Do we need resources to brainstorm and 'ideate'?

- Will we need space for breakout sessions?
- Do we need power and wi-fi for participants' laptops?
- Should we take the meeting offsite to aid concentration?

5. When
Work the timing

Now we have sorted out the *why*, *what* and *who*, we are in a position to set the *when*. Your schedule, and those of the key participants, will have a great influence here. Any deadlines and time sensitivity relating to agenda items will also be critical.

It is important to give people as much notice as possible when requesting a chunk of their time. Last-minute meetings, or meetings scheduled for the next day, can throw other people's plans into chaos. Avoid this if at all possible.

As to the meeting length, the agenda that you have created should determine this. How long will each item likely need, allowing for the fudge factor? If it looks like the meeting will be too long, can the agenda be shortened? Are there items that could be dealt with another way or at another time?

Remember, we are aiming to reduce the length of our meetings by 25 per cent, so a short, effective meeting will achieve more than a long, ineffective one.

It is worth considering placing time constraints on each agenda item, allocating the number of minutes that can be spent on the item. This will create a sense of focus for all attendees before and during the meeting.

The agenda timing will also serve as a critical tool to help the meeting convenor to keep on track. Once the allocated time for an agenda item is used up, the convenor should note this and direct the group to make a decision about whether they stay with the item at the expense of other items or place it in a parking lot to be dealt with further outside the meeting. A prioritised agenda will help with this decision making.

Many of the meeting problems we discussed at the start of this chapter can be reduced if we bring a consistent, robust meeting planning process to the team. The process outlined here forces productive behaviours, which result in productive meetings.

Be prepared

Qualities: *Purposeful, Reliable, Mindful*

Make the time to prepare for meetings, whether you are the meeting organiser or simply a participant. Plan and anticipate upcoming meetings, and schedule time to prepare ahead of the meeting.

Invest time to plan. If a meeting is worth holding, it is worth planning. A general rule of thumb is to invest 20 per cent of the meeting duration on planning the event. This of course should be done *before* the meeting. So for a 45-minute meeting, plan on spending at least ten minutes on planning.

Don't you think those you have invited to attend deserve this effort given the investment of their precious time?

EXPERT INTERVIEW
Donna McGeorge—on effective meetings

Donna McGeorge and I are very much in agreement on meetings in the corporate workplace. Donna is the author of *Making Work Work*, and meetings are one of the specific areas in which she counsels her corporate clients. Her upcoming book is titled *The 25-Minute Meeting*.

Firstly, we agree that most people spend too much time in meetings.

I remember an executive in one global manufacturing organisation I worked with talking to a group of new managers. He warned them, 'We believe you could spend your whole career in this company just going from one meeting to another, and never actually doing anything besides meetings and conversations.'

One of Donna's frustrations is a common overreliance on PowerPoint presentations in meetings. She finds that a lot of people are invited to meetings as spectators and have to sit there reading slide after slide. You don't always need slides to have a conversation or make a decision, she insists, and the effort that goes into creating those slides and the time the slides take up in the meeting can make them a very poor investment.

Donna challenges the efficiency of bringing people together for meeting after meeting. She provides a good example of game theory productivity in meetings.

> *I sometimes think we call a meeting when maybe five phone calls might be more efficient. We could have a meeting that goes for an hour, with five participants. That may feel efficient because we are all there at the same time. And it may be efficient for the meeting organiser, but it's not efficient for the participants, because I could just do a five- or ten-minute phone call with each of those individuals, which would still be an hour of my time, but only five or ten minutes of theirs.*

We also agree that punctuality is non-negotiable. And punctual means five minutes early, not just on time. Yet we both work in many organisations where being late is just part of the territory.

> *I heard a story in one of my client companies about a new manager who was trying to create a culture of punctuality. They would lock the door at the meeting start time. There would be people knocking on the door asking to come in, and the manager would say, 'No, you can't come in.'*

> *The next meeting would take place and some people would come on time because they had learned at the last meeting that you're going to get locked out if you don't. But they would then start second-guessing some of the decisions made at the previous week's meeting. The manager would then say, 'No, you weren't here. You don't get a say in that.'*

> *Pretty quickly people started to show up on time because they knew that there was just going to be no tolerance for being late. I love it.*

Donna's big three ideas for effective meetings are *punctuality, preparation* and *presence*. Be on time, prepare adequately and be engaged in the meeting. None of this is rocket science. It is basic stuff that we all know but we don't put into practice consistently enough.

Running an awesome meeting

So, once we have made absolutely sure the meeting is warranted, the right people have been invited, the right amount of time is allocated and the right resources have been made available, it is time to run our meeting and make sure it is an awesome experience for everyone involved!

Whoever is responsible for running the meeting needs to make sure it achieves its intended outcomes. Everyone should not only leave on time, but they should leave with a clear idea of what needs to happen after the meeting so that whatever was created, decided, or discussed does not go to waste.

The person who runs the meeting should not necessarily be the boss, or the most senior person. Many teams rotate this responsibility, or leave it up to the most appropriate person for the job. A project meeting that involves a senior sponsor may be better run by the project manager, who is probably across the details of the project more than the sponsor, no matter how senior they are.

An awesome meeting has three phases, but these phases are not equally distributed when it comes to time. A percentage breakdown of 10/80/10 works well in this situation.

1. **Focus the attendees—10 per cent.** The first phase involves focusing the attendees on the agenda. This is the plan for the meeting, and it is worth reminding attendees of what needs to be covered and achieved. Begin with the meeting objectives. Remember that even though you put a huge amount of work into creating a productive agenda, some attendees may not have read it (I know!), so let's get everyone on the same page.

2. **Manage the agenda—80 per cent.** The second phase is about keeping things on track. Someone needs to keep an eye on time and make sure that agenda items don't run over, or if they do, the group is made aware and the agenda is reprioritised. The meeting chair, for want of a better term, also needs to manage the personalities in the room and try to keep people on topic and on an even keel. Play the issue, not the person, as they say. If new issues arise, it is worth using a parking lot on a whiteboard to capture what needs to be taken offline or dealt with in the next meeting.

3. **Confirm next steps—10 per cent.** The final phase is about wrapping up efficiently and clearly. Everyone should walk away with a clear understanding of the actions they have committed to and by when, and be accountable to those actions. Taking a few minutes at the end to go over each action and who is responsible will increase the chances of productive traction after the meeting.

In *Smart Work* I discussed how Tony Hall, one of my training team, talks about planning your day like a chef plans cooking a meal. There is the preparation, the cooking, and the clean-up afterwards. Each phase is critical to a great meal being created. Your meetings are no different.

Mindful interruptions

Is this a weird place to talk about interruptions—in the middle of a chapter on meetings? No, I reckon it is the perfect place. If you think about it, an interruption *is* a meeting, just an unplanned one! And it needs to be managed in the appropriate way if we are to be productive.

In *Smart Work*, I discussed the three modes that we need to operate in to minimise unnecessary interruptions. They were *lockdown mode*, *focus mode* and *available mode*. But there I was focused on strategies to minimise the disruption caused when someone interrupts you.

How do we reduce the disruption we potentially cause others by interrupting them unnecessarily?

Here are some things to consider before you interrupt others:

- **Interrupt with purpose.** The first step is to interrupt with purpose. Don't just interrupt because you have thought of a question and spotted the person to ask. Think about whether it is critical to this moment, and if not, park it for later. If you do interrupt, make sure your thinking is clear, and you know exactly what you want to ask.

- **Have a strategy to capture discussion thoughts.** Most interruptions happen when they happen because we don't have a good solution for capturing discussion items. Do your colleagues a favour and devise one. Whether you dedicate a page in your notebook to them or capture voice memos on your phone, make sure you have a 'friction-free' strategy in place.

- **Put yourself in their shoes.** Try to short-circuit your normal interruption behaviours. As you go to interrupt, try to put yourself in their shoes. Observe what they are doing. What is their body language? What is their reaction as you interrupt? Maybe give them an out. When I am on a break during training that I am running, I really appreciate when people interrupt me to ask a question, but suggest that it could wait until after my break. They anticipate that I might be busy, or needing a rest.

The following are four strategies you can use to help train your team in a better practice around interruptions.

1. **Advertise open times.** If you are a busy senior executive, you may feel 'set upon' when you do appear at your desk, because you are mostly in meetings, and everyone wants a piece of you. Start by advertising two or three 'available' hours in your week, when you are happy for anyone to come and see you. Book a meeting room, and send out a note each week, and you will become the most available

manager in the organisation. The funny thing is, most people won't take advantage of this option, but they will feel better that it is there!

2. **Set a time limit.** If someone does need to interrupt you, set a clear time limit. People often ask if you have a minute, then take 30. Tell them you have five minutes (or however long you feel is appropriate), and insist they stay focused on the one issue in that time.

3. **Use focusing questions.** If an interruption starts to get unfocused, refocus the discussion by using a focusing question. One of my mentors will often stop me in mid sentence and ask, 'What is the question you need to ask me, to help me to help you?' This is a powerful way to stop someone reeling off their life story as background, when it does not really add value. Sometimes too much context is counterproductive.

4. **But don't just kill collaboration.** Don't dismiss interruptions. They are an important part of how we interact and work, and help create a social bond within the team. Remember that one of the interruption modes discussed in *Smart Work* is available mode. If you are doing low-level tasks such as email, by all means stop and chat when interrupted. If you bump into someone on the stairs, take the opportunity to discuss the project you are both working on.

But try to reduce unnecessary interruptions that stop people focusing on concentrated work.

Interrupt mindfully

Qualities: *Purposeful, Mindful*

Most interruptions happen because you think of something when you see someone, and you don't want to miss the opportunity. So you interrupt. If it is not urgent, capture the thought for discussion at a more suitable time.

So, that was a brief interruption about interruptions. Now, back to our chapter on meetings!

Are all agenda items the same?

Some meetings will have a single focus, but many will have a variety of agenda items to be discussed, each requiring a different approach. When planning the agenda, clarifying each type of agenda item will help you to focus on what you need to do to cover that item most efficiently and effectively.

Most meetings will involve up to four types of agenda items, as shown in figure 5.2.

Figure 5.2: meeting agenda types

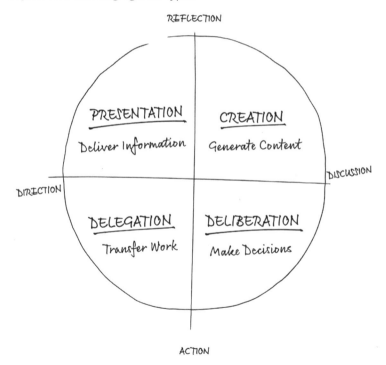

1. Creation
Brainstorming, planning or ideation

The Creation meeting agenda type sees ideas generated and captured through brainstorming. Many brainstorming processes have been documented, but generally they follow a divergent/convergent pattern: a range of ideas are generated, then these are assessed, prioritised and narrowed down to a shortlist. Planning and creative exercises are sometimes called *ideation*.

When we are meeting to generate ideas, options, plans or strategies, the key focus should be on the process used to create and capture the content. Creation needs to be facilitated, especially with larger groups. As the meeting organiser, you may not have strong skills in this area, so you may need to bring someone in who has the skills or ask another meeting participant to lead the discussion.

2. Deliberation
Decisions, approvals or recommendations

A second agenda item type is Deliberation, in which a decision needs to be made. Here a group, preferably a small one, discusses an issue and comes to a decision. The key is the number of participants involved, as the research shows that too many participants makes decision making harder and can dilute the focus. Discussions about approvals and recommendations are also part of the deliberation family.

When making decisions in meetings, having the right people in the room is key. We need to ensure that the actual decision makers are present. It can be extremely frustrating to arrive at a meeting only to find that the decision maker has had to pull out, rendering the meeting pointless. It is also important to ensure the right people are in the room to provide the data and information necessary to the decision making.

There is a school of thought that we should not use meetings to make decisions. In his book *Read This Before Our Next Meeting*, Al Pittampalli argues that managers need to step up and be accountable for making decisions, rather than calling meetings for the purpose. He suggests that these meetings can be a way for managers to avoid accountability and responsibility for the decision. If it goes wrong, they can say that 'we all made that decision'.

Al suggests that one of the functions of a modern meeting is to support decisions already made. We make decisions outside of the meeting, and come together if necessary to ratify or debate a decision already made. It is an interesting position, and while I am a little hesitant to wholeheartedly recommend this approach, I feel that, used in the right way, this could save many hours of wasteful meetings.

3. Delegation
Team tasks, requests or resource allocation

A third agenda item type is Delegation. This is often done one-on-one, with a task delegated or assigned to another person. It can of course also happen in a larger meeting. To my mind, discussions about resource allocation in projects also fall under the umbrella of delegation, as do work requests from other departments, suppliers or clients.

One of the biggest issues with delegation meetings is that they simply don't happen. So much of our work is delegated on the fly. The delegation is not planned effectively, and often happens at the person's desk or in the hallway.

When the agenda item is to transfer work to another person, the focus should be on setting clear expectations. This means some thought needs to go into the delegation, with the task, deadlines and expected quality communicated clearly. It is a good idea to clarify the capacity needed and allow room for negotiation.

In chapter 7, I talk to Scott Stein about a wonderfully effective delegation process that gets a better result every time.

4. Presentation
Briefing, update or speech

Finally, there is the Presentation agenda type. This covers a broad range of offerings, from sales pitches to large group presentations by senior management. This agenda item tends to be unidirectional, perhaps with some discussion, depending on the presentation group size. Presentations can also include briefings and progress updates.

One of the things that reduces productivity when dealing with a presentation item is death by PowerPoint. I am all for visuals, and use PowerPoint presentations in all of my training sessions. But I don't create documents in slide form and force people to read them or, even worse, listen to me reading them.

The focus of a presentation item should be on the needs of the audience. How do you help them to best digest and understand the information being presented?

Whether it is a large group presentation or a one-on-one sales pitch, your message will gain greater traction if it is framed with the needs of the listener in mind.

Focus your meeting with an agenda

A useful way to help your team develop good practices around your meetings is to adopt a meeting agenda template, encouraging everyone to use it for every meeting.

Using a template forces consistency and keeps us honest. Empty fields show others where we have been a bit slack, so we feel more obligated to fill them out! Using a template until it becomes a familiar format makes it easier for others to digest the meeting information.

Figure 5.3 show a sample meeting agenda template that was designed in MS OneNote. It is a simple set of tables, but it clearly displays the required information and encourages the meeting strategies outlined in this chapter.

Another good strategy for an agenda template is to create it in MS Word, then copy it into an email signature in MS Outlook. It can then be inserted into a meeting invitation whenever you need it.

Figure 5.3: a meeting agenda template

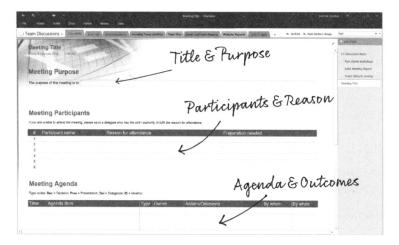

As you can see, the agenda sample in figure 5.3 follows the 5W meeting planning process outlined earlier in this chapter. There is space to clearly outline the meeting purpose. There is a section devoted to creating the agenda and including additional information that provides context for the meeting participants. You can then use the fields in the meeting invitation form to set the who, when and where.

Busy people need help to do the right thing. Templates keep us honest, because it is immediately obvious to ourselves and others if there are areas we have not adequately prepared for.

Focus your meetings

Qualities: *Purposeful, Punctual*

Ensure meetings achieve their intended outcomes and finish on time by using a properly prepared agenda. You will maximise the time commitment of everyone involved if you take the time to prepare before the meeting.

EXPERT INTERVIEW
Lynne Cazaly — on ideation

Creation is a type of agenda item we often have to manage in meetings. We need to create ideas, plans and strategies to achieve our objectives. Brainstorming is the most common process applied in meetings to facilitate group creation or, as it is often called, *ideation*.

Sadly, many teams use a narrow range of marginally effective techniques to generate and create. For example, linear processes such as list making using a flip chart are often employed. I have my doubts that this really gets the creative juices going as it should, so I talked to Lynne Cazaly, author of *Leader as Facilitator*, among other books.

Lynne specialises in helping teams to boost engagement and collaboration, and is an expert on ideation.

When we talked about creation activities in meetings, Lynne's first point was that too often managers call meetings and just expect the attendees to be able to create on demand, which is a tough ask for most people. She suggests attendees need to be primed, just as an old-fashioned water pump or engine needs to be primed before it will start.

> Next week I'll be running a massive ideation session with 70 people for a local council, and we're trying to generate some really incredible ideas for the future. Now, people are going to show up, and I'm not just going to stand there with a flip chart at the front of the ring. I've got a very detailed process that I will go through to prime them to deliver some of the best ideas.
>
> I imagine the most socially anxious or introverted person in the room and I make sure that I'm designing something they'll feel comfortable with. So I'm going to be more likely to get input and contributions from everyone because they feel safe in that space to give their ideas, and if they're primed well they're more likely to come up with good stuff.

Priming takes preparation. The first step is to send out an agenda and highlight any 'creation' agenda items. Lynne suggests posing two or three questions that will be discussed in the meeting. This primes people by getting them thinking before the event.

Lynne recommends the use of visual aids, even in virtual meetings. This helps people to not just capture content, but to 'hear' it.

'Visuals help people hear each other, especially when they are in remote and distributed in network teams.'

Unlike decision making, which suffers from too many people being involved, creation can be done comfortably with bigger groups if approached in the right way.

> *Trying to create in what I call a whole group—that is, with everyone focused on one activity—can be a challenge. But if I was to break down a group of 25 into five groups of five, I would have a better chance of generating some quality content. Now I'm going to have a more generative, productive outcome.*
>
> *I will be doing this with the group next week. At times during the day I will break the group down so we can generate quantity, or what I call 'plenty'. Break the group down to generate lots of ideas, then bring them back to the whole group again.*

When creating ideas or options, Lynn believes, it is very important to generate quantity, with no filters or criticism, using a 'divergent' strategy to come up with lots of ideas. You can then run a 'convergent' activity to prioritise the results or narrow down the choices to the best few. I personally love doing this visually with sticky notes on walls or whiteboards, as they are colourful and can be easily rearranged.

Lynne's advice for effective ideation, in a nutshell, is *prepare*, *process* and *plenty*. Prepare before the meeting and prime the participants, have a process in mind to facilitate the creation, and go for lots and lots of ideas.

If we overlay our productivity values on this, to approach creation in this way is to be *purposeful* and *mindful*. You approach the activity with purpose, rather than just turning up and hoping for the best. And you are mindful of the participants' needs, helping them to contribute most effectively.

6

COLLABORATE: MAKE PROJECTS GREAT

If you are not a project manager by trade, you could be forgiven for believing your role does not require you to plan and manage projects. Some of us think of projects as those big things that large teams work on over a period of years to deliver major products, outcomes or change.

We all work on projects. Every day of every week, consciously or not.

Projects are one of the most common ways we collaborate with one another in the workplace. Any discrete piece of work that requires several steps to complete is a project. Writing a report is a project. Planning a team offsite is a project. Developing a marketing brochure is a project. Alongside our everyday work, projects are how we get stuff done.

I recently presented at the National Partner Conference for one of the big consulting firms in Australia. The keynote address by their COO was electric. His challenge was to inspire 800 partners, who all owned their own little piece of the business, to persuade them to collaborate more and share information for the good of the client and of the firm.

One of their medium-term goals was to achieve number one market leadership in Australia. But, he explained, they could only attain that together, rather than individually. They had to get better at collaborating on opportunities and projects. I think this is true for many organisations.

This chapter is not designed to be a how-to guide to project management. Instead, my focus is on the smaller projects that most of us are engaged in at work. I want to explore ways to collaborate on projects in a more productive way.

Collaboration has become a bit of a buzzword. Over the past few years, physical workspaces have been redesigned to promote and encourage us to work together in a more flexible and interactive way. Activity-based workplaces (ABW) are all the rage, with collaborative spaces designed to help workers find the right space for the type of activity they are engaged in. This might be an individual workspace one day, a project team table the next.

While the jury is still out on whether activity-based workplaces actually increase collaboration, or simply save floor space and overheads, I do believe they increase productivity in the long run. (And as a consultant who visits many different business offices, I love these bright, funky and flexible workspaces, which are always a hive of positive activity.)

Wherever and however you work, collaboration is critical to success in today's competitive marketplace.

Effective collaboration, however, is complex. It has many elements that need to come together to make collaboration flow, including environment, teamwork, systems and tools, and indeed the wider culture. All these considerations contribute to and reinforce productive collaboration.

Alignment, agreement and awareness

Life would be simpler in many ways if we had a job where we could work alone, in perfect isolation. Sure, we would need to be self-motivated, and to enjoy our own company, but we would not have to deal with many of the issues and complexities that arise from working with other people in a busy, complex organisation.

As we have discussed, when we work with others we tend to create friction that drags productivity down. There are many strategies that can help to oil the cogs and reduce the collaboration friction that happens when we work together, especially on projects.

Underpinning these strategies are three ingredients that dictate the success or failure of productive collaboration within a team, as shown in figure 6.1.

Figure 6.1: elements of collaboration

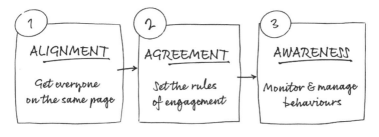

1. Alignment
Get everyone on the same page

A successful sporting team displays a high level of alignment on the field. Of course both teams are aligned in wanting to win, but the main alignment in a high-level sporting team is in the way they play.

A great coach will create a vision for the team, and show them how to execute that vision through a particular style of play and a set of specific strategies. The team who are on the same page and execute that vision on game day are likely to be the winning team.

As a team, whether you work together every day, or come together for a specific project, being aligned on what needs to be achieved is critical. It creates a platform for collaborating successfully. Without alignment, you will have people with different, possibly competing priorities pulling in different directions.

In the workplace, when we are aligned, work just gets easier. It is easier to plan and prioritise, even when priorities change or conflict. Work tends to be less reactive and more proactive. It becomes easier to negotiate with others because we are all clear about the objectives.

Being on the same page is a great analogy for alignment. It means we all have a common understanding of what we are trying to achieve and how we are going to achieve it.

Are you on the same page as your colleagues and team members when you collaborate? Or are you sometimes focused on achieving one thing while your colleagues are focused on another?

Alignment comes from a shared vision. As leaders, we need to make sure everyone understands what needs to be achieved, and why it is important. We cannot take it for granted that people will get this. We must explicitly discuss the vision and purpose at the start of any project or collaboration.

In his book *Projectify*, Jeff Schwisow talks about the power of purpose:

When you connect your people's strategic efforts to a higher business purpose, you give them an understanding of the business impact they're having. You allow them to see that their work is contributing to meaningful progress for the organisation. This motivates them to do more—to keep making progress and adjust their activities to be as meaningful as possible. This progress drives creativity in solving the business's strategic problems. It also enhances the level of collaboration that exists across your business but, most importantly, exists in the cross-functional project teams you establish to take on these problems.

By sharing the purpose of the project, and the specific outcomes that need to be achieved, your team will not only be more inspired to do the work—they will make better decisions. If they are aligned, they are more likely to plan and manage actions proactively, and will be better positioned to make priority decisions. They are also more likely to prepare for project meetings and turn up on time.

When we are busy, and are not aligned on our objectives, we get slack, we make poor decisions and we leave things until the last minute more frequently.

Seek clarification

Qualities: *Purposeful, Reliable*

Don't be afraid to ask for clarification if you are uncertain about what you are meant to be doing. If you don't do so, the ramifications for all involved can be serious. So if you are not sure, ask questions until you are.

2. Agreement
Set the rules of engagement

Once we are aligned on what we need to achieve, we need to agree how we will work together in the most productive way. Chapter 2 outlines some qualities that support our working together successfully. But some collaborations may need more specific agreements to minimise friction and drag.

Agreements should be made both on how we will work together and on the tools we will use to collaborate.

One of the best ways to increase team productivity is to embrace an effective set of collaboration tools and use them consistently to make our work and progress visible.

If we also agree on how we will communicate, meet, raise issues and update progress we will have set the ground rules for productive collaboration. Because our work is complex and we are all busy, this may not completely eradicate productivity friction within the team, but it will minimise it.

I often work with teams that have come together for a specific project and will break up at the end of that project. While they often spend a lot of time and effort getting clear about the work that needs to be done, they rarely have a conversation about how they will work together.

It is often assumed that we know how best to work with one another. We just work the way we always work. But time spent agreeing on some basic ground rules on how we will work together will save a lot of time in the thick of the project.

Here are some examples of effective working agreements for a project:

- We agree to minimise email noise and aim to talk directly rather than using email to work stuff out.
- We agree to schedule a stand-up, 15-minute meeting twice a week to discuss progress.
- We decide to use a shared OneNote notebook to collate all critical project information and meeting notes.

Such ground rules will not completely eradicate unproductive situations, but they will minimise them.

Do what you say you will

Qualities: *Reliable, Mindful*

If you commit to something, follow through and deliver, or renegotiate if necessary. Your brand is tarnished every time you don't do what you say. People want to work with people they can rely on.

---

3. Awareness
Monitor and manage behaviours

Once we have aligned ourselves and agreed on how we will work, we need to ensure we follow through on our agreements by monitoring our collaborations and adjusting any disruptive behaviours.

By applying 'game theory productivity' thinking to our collaborations, we can elevate our awareness so we view all our collaborations from the perspective of both our own effectiveness and the productivity of the people we work with.

Building our awareness takes time and effort. But if we approach every day and every interaction in a mindful way, we create a new mindset and a new way of working quickly.

A good way of helping your team become more aware is to build it into project meetings. Meet regularly to discuss project progress, and take some time to check in and see if there are any productivity frictions that are dragging people down.

Are our meetings effective and relevant? Are we sending too many emails? Is the work and progress visible to everyone? Simple questions such as these, asked regularly, raise awareness and put team productivity *permanently* on the agenda.

EXPERT INTERVIEW
Matt Lumsdaine—on mindfulness

When we work with other people, which is most of the time, there is a huge risk of distraction. As we have discussed, mindfulness is one of the four key productivity qualities that we are aiming to embrace. I caught up with Matt Lumsdaine, a corporate coach, trainer and expert in mindfulness and attention management, to discuss how we can be more mindful in our work.

Matt works with managers and their teams to help them to focus in often very distracting workspaces. The first thing we need to do when working together, he suggests, is to adopt both an 'attention in' mindset and an 'attention out' mindset. And if we want to manage our attention we need to be able to operate on both levels.

An analogy that I might draw is our national rugby team. We know that each of the individuals who get to pull on the national jersey must be very good at what they do. And if you watch them, their attention to detail, their attention to their craft and their individual skill level is evident. This is 'attention in' at work.

But the team won't perform well unless there's another form of attention at work, and that is 'attention out'. When the team is working well, you know that individuals are anticipating what other members of the team are doing and what's required. It's like they know the next move.

So it's about two aspects of attention—one focused on your own task, and the other open to understanding what's required by the team as a whole.

This is such an important skill in the modern workplace. Building awareness about our attention and how to manage it helps us to work together as a team. We also need to know when to put more emphasis on 'attention in' rather than 'attention out'. Sometimes we need to concentrate on a piece of work, to lock ourselves away in a meeting room for an hour to remove the risk of distraction.

At other times we need to collaborate closely with others, being mindful of their needs as well as our own.

We discussed the issue of distraction in open-plan workplaces. Today we do not have offices as we might have had in the good old days. Often we don't even have cubicles. For the most part we work in open-plan or activity-based workplaces that are designed to promote collaboration, though some would argue they mainly promote distraction! So how do we manage our attention in this environment?

Matt suggests there are three main distractions to guard against. Firstly, there are electronic distractions such as email and instant messaging alerts. No surprise that he recommends turning these off and checking your communications at regular times.

Secondly, there are the personal distractions—the ones in our own heads that we allow to push into our conscious mind to distract us. My solution to these distractions is to set up a system to capture thoughts and mind clutter for later. Write it down, send yourself an email, make a voice recording—just capture it somehow and get back to what you were doing!

Finally, there are human interruptions. These are hard to avoid completely, but Matt recommends using some sort of visual sign that indicates you are trying to concentrate. This should make most people think twice before interrupting. Of course, there is always the good old headphones strategy.

One of the problems with being interrupted, Matt suggests, is that we try to deal with the interruption without stopping our own work, which means we end up feeling stressed and resentful. His solution is simple.

> *A technique I teach is called 'intentional switching'. If an interruption or distraction is inevitable, or has occurred, you can do one of two things. Either stop what you are doing and give your full attention to the person who has interrupted you. Focus on whatever it is they want to talk about, complete that conversation and then go back to your previous task.*

Or you can stop and face them intentionally, and say something along the lines of, 'I am working on something really important at the moment. Could this wait for half an hour until I can give you my full attention?'

The key is to be intentional with your strategy, rather than trying to multitask and getting frustrated.

Being mindful in a team environment takes active commitment to reduce unproductive distraction and interruption. Matt recommends starting each day by setting your intention. Remind yourself each morning that your aim is to work productively and to serve others in a productive way.

The enemy of intention, he explains, is busyness, so as we progress through a busy day, we need to pause periodically to 'anchor' ourselves and to slow down a bit to get more done.

I think it's really important to take the time to pause or to stop. It's very simple. Anchor the mind in the present moment. You can do that by just sitting at your desk and feeling the weight of your body on the chair. Or even just resting your hands on the desktop and feeling the surface of the desk, and focusing your attention on some sensory input.

Because, while the mind's great at racing off at a crazy pace, the body lives in the present. So anchoring in the present, even if only for 30 seconds, can have an amazing impact on our mental state. I know from personal experience, and from feedback from hundreds and hundreds of people I've trained to do this, that the additional space and the sense of energy you can achieve from something as simple as that is amazing.

Finally, Matt and I talked about rituals to start the day in a mindful and productive way, to prepare the mind for a hectic day. For him, a few minutes of meditation is the key. Some time spent meditating gives you a mental fitness that serves you through the day.

When I speak of mental fitness, I'm really referring to our ability to take control of where our attention goes. Shakespeare said the mind makes a terrible master but a wonderful servant.

Most of us are at the whim of our mind: wherever it goes we follow it. Learning to manage that through a meditation practice is really powerful. And there are plenty of ways of doing so, plenty of ways of meditating.

Ultimately, someone who can manage their attention effectively can be far more productive than someone who is prone to distraction and a victim of their environment. They will also be a more productive team player.

Collaborate mindfully

Qualities: *Mindful*

Always think about the productivity of the group when collaborating. Remember, the best results come from doing what is best for you and the group at the same time. Treat others the way you would like to be treated.

Project collaboration: make them visible

Projects must be among the most complex endeavours we get involved in at work. Long timeframes, multiple resources, big budgets, a high profile, big risks and lots of moving parts—and all this on top of your day job!

Then there are the smaller endeavours: reports, mailouts, team events. These are projects too. They might not be as complex, but they still have moving parts and deadlines.

The good news is that projects are just complex tasks, and they generally involve activities we work on together. So if we apply the right framework and approach to our projects, we will achieve great things.

**Projects are the key to getting meaningful work done
in any organisation.**

So how can we ensure that we collaborate on projects productively? I won't outline a complete project management process here — there are people who are far more qualified than I am to do that. Instead, I will provide a simple framework for thinking about your project work to ensure effective collaboration.

The purpose of this framework is to make the moving parts in your project more visible. When we paint a picture of the project, and hang it where everyone can see it, we create clarity and understanding.

If we revisit the 5W cooperation framework, we can apply four of the W questions to projects. *Why*, *what*, *when* and *who* are the key questions to ask when planning or managing any project, as shown in figure 6.2. Answering these questions helps to make the project visible to you and to all of the stakeholders.

Figure 6.2: the why, what, when and who of projects

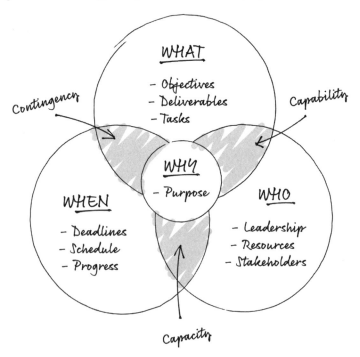

1. Start with WHY
Clarify the purpose

As so often in life, and in this book, you must start with *why*. Make sure you and your team are clear about the purpose of the project, and how it will help you to achieve your required business outcomes.

Remember that projects are the most impactful way to get meaningful work done in your organisation, but they also demand a high price. They take a lot of time, energy and money. So make sure your projects are relevant and linked to your business outcomes. You are better off choosing a few projects wisely, and delivering on these, than spreading yourself too thin.

Ask yourself the following questions to really understand *why*:

- Why are we doing this project?

- What business outcome does this project link to?

- What will the project achieve in terms of business outcomes?

- What is the opportunity cost in doing this project? What will we not do as a result?

- Is this the best use of our time, energy, money and resources?

- What parts of the organisation will be affected by the project?

2. Get clear about WHAT
Objectives, deliverables and tasks

Now we get to the nitty-gritty of the project. What exactly needs to be done? A project is essentially a bunch of tasks that have to be completed. You could just create a task list but, if you are collaborating with others, this list will need to have some structure and order to make it understandable.

When generating the project actions, it is a good idea to start at a high level before zooming in to finer levels of granularity. The first step is to define the project objectives.

Clearly identifying the project objectives helps to identify what needs to be done.

The objectives describe what will be different after the project's completion. What issue will be resolved? What new system will be in place? What product will be brought to market? This is a part of the alignment process discussed earlier in the chapter, and is an important part of getting everyone on the same page.

Once you have outlined the project objectives, you can start to define the project deliverables. These are the physical or tangible outputs the project will deliver. They could be an actual product or tool, or they could be a change to a business process. For example, in a project to design a new productivity training program, one deliverable might be the training workbooks, another the slide presentation, and yet another the marketing collateral. These are all physical deliverables within the project.

Deliverables are useful, because they provide a contextual way to organise the project tasks. They also provide an easy way to understand if a stage of the project is complete. Has that deliverable in fact been delivered?

Once you have a list of deliverables, you can start to generate the task list that might sit under each deliverable. What are all the things that need to be done before you can say the deliverable has been completed? This list of actions under each deliverable is often called a *work breakdown structure*. It provides a total list of things that need to be done. Later we will look at what this looks like in practice.

---

3. Decide WHO needs to be involved
Leadership, resources and stakeholders

Many informal projects are run like day-to-day operational work. We just whip off a few emails to people asking for stuff to be done, without taking the time to think about who needs to be fully involved with the project and how this should be communicated.

But project success depends on the people involved in the project. We need to involve them, communicate with them, inspire them and lead them if we want them to be interested in delivering a great project.

'Who' begins at the leadership level. Identifying who the project manager and the project sponsor will be is critical. The project manager has responsibility for running the project and the project team. The project sponsor usually approves the finances and can cancel or greenlight the project. The sponsor is also the link between the project team and senior management. Projects without a proper sponsor often fail, or are sidelined when things get busy or tight.

Of course, the project team also needs to be identified and brought on board. Choose people who are interested and have the capabilities and the capacity to take the project on. Look back at figure 6.2 and you'll see that capability and capacity are the key considerations where *what* and *who* intersect, and where *when* and *who* intersect.

A project may have a range of stakeholders who need to have input, to be kept up to date and, at the end of the project, to be satisfied with the outcome. Stakeholders may include management, end users, suppliers, technical experts, government bodies or other parts of the business that may be touched indirectly by the project.

It is important to have a plan in place to communicate with stakeholders, even on small projects. So the first step is to identify the stakeholders for the project, then ensure you communicate regularly with this important group.

---

4. Work out WHEN
Schedule, milestones and progress

You are now in a position to think about the *when*. Your starting point should be to identify any hard deadlines that must be met. These may become constraints in the project, and may take some creative work to achieve.

Complex projects can get very convoluted when it comes to managing deadlines and schedules. I won't even pretend that this book does project scheduling justice. But you do need to think about *when* from a collaboration perspective.

Too many projects are run on the fly, with tasks allocated and deadlines identified, but no real control over when work should be started or how long tasks might take.

If a project task is delegated with a due date but is then buried in someone's inbox, there is a real risk it will be left until the last minute, causing stress or even a missed deadline.

The amount of detail to go into with scheduling and timing will depend on the size and complexity of the project. Complex projects drawing on many resources may need a schedule that incorporates project tasks, milestones, start dates, finish dates, durations, resource allocation and task dependencies. These all work together to create a dynamic visual picture of the project schedule, and allow the project manager to manage resourcing, as well as any schedule delays.

Simpler projects might just need no more than an Excel spreadsheet with bars indicating roughly when each task should start and finish. This is a lot simpler to use but is a much blunter tool. Project delays will not be as readily picked up, and the implications of delays on the project deadlines might not be apparent. This is why there must be frequent communication on the progress of work in the project.

The project manager should check in regularly with the team on progress, issues and possible delays. Rather than asking how much work has been done on a task, a better question is how much work is still left to do. This provides a more accurate picture of where you stand, especially given that the final 10 per cent of a project task can take as long as the first 90 per cent.

Taking the time, as a team, to understand the *why*, *what*, *who* and *when* of a project will help you to collaborate on that project much more productively. I know you are busy, but there cannot be any shortcuts here. You are too busy *not* to do this.

Own your work

Qualities: *Purposeful, Reliable*

Be accountable for your deliverables and outcomes. This means taking ownership of your schedule, your priorities and your time. Don't make the excuse that you were busy—we are all busy.

Now we have explored the key elements that need to be considered when planning a project, what about the right tools to manage the work and progress? Let's look at the best tool for the job.

The best tool for the job

What is the best tool to use to manage our project work? This is one of the questions I am most often asked when running team productivity training sessions. The question frequently comes from managers or workers who are not dedicated project managers, but are still expected to manage projects and complex work as a part of their role.

Essentially, as we have seen, projects are a bunch of actions that, when completed, will achieve the desired outcome or deliverables. This means we are juggling a number of different tasks at different times, which is more complex than simply dealing with your inbox.

Our brain can remember lots of things, and understand difficult concepts, but it often struggles to recall the things we need to do at the right time.

To prevent our projects from stalling or running over time or over budget, we need to plan and proactively manage these activities. Above all, we need tools to help us manage the complexity of project work.

Another factor that makes most project work different from much of our day-to-day operational work is the fact that multiple other people may be working on the same project, so we need a way to collaborate on this work. This adds a layer of complexity that we need to manage.

Not all projects need complex project management software. This is where a lot of people go wrong and end up having to learn how to project manage their project management tools! In most cases a high-end planning tool such as MS Project is overkill. I see lots of people installing project management software, then getting so bogged down in learning how to use it that they either give up or use it ineffectively.

So how do you figure out what tools to use and when to use them? Figure 6.3 may help.

Figure 6.3: which tool, when?

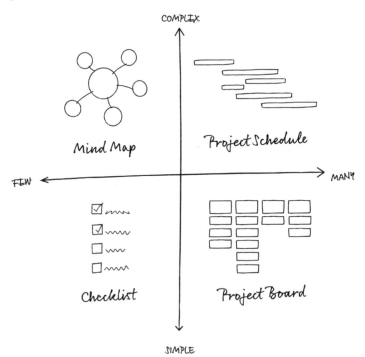

Project scheduling tools

If a project is complex, and has many people working on it, you probably need to consider using a full-blown project management tool such as MS Project. (Of course, there are many project management applications in the marketplace. MS Project is probably the most well-known and possibly the most accessible.)

MS Project provides different views to help you and your team to visualise the project. The most familiar for most people is the Gantt chart view, which shows the project tasks scheduled on a timeline. MS Project allows you to add dependencies to each task so you can understand if one task needs to be completed before another can start, or whether there is the potential to schedule tasks concurrently so they can be worked on at the same time.

Concurrency is an especially useful concept if you have multiple people working on the project, as of course these resources can be working on different tasks at once. It is not so easy when you are the only resource, though, as you can only do one thing at a time.

This is why a tool such as MS Project is a good choice with complex projects with multiple resources, as you can shorten the project timeframes by using concurrent scheduling.

The challenge can be that it takes a lot of work and experience to plan and schedule a project properly using a tool such as this. There is a lot of room for error if you are updating information in a complex relational diagram. If you do not understand the implications of the changes you make to your schedule, you can very quickly end up with an incorrect view of your project's status or progress. Rubbish in, rubbish out.

So think carefully before you use a tool like MS Project. If you feel your projects warrant it or something similar, get some training or ensure you have access to someone in the team who knows what they are doing.

Many people turn to Microsoft Excel to create simple project schedules or Gantt chart views for the project tasks. While this is a blunter instrument to use, it is effective and much, much simpler when working on smaller projects.

Mind maps

Mind mapping is a technique developed by Tony Buzan in the 1970s to visualise complex information. It uses a tree format with a central topic hosting branches, which in turn host sub-branches. These connections are often called parent/child relationships.

A mind map allows you to break down a complex project into several main chunks, with the tasks and activities that sit under each chunk forming natural groups. This makes it easy to visualise the whole project, and to zoom in and out of different levels of detail as needed.

If the project is complex but you are working on it alone or with only one or two others in the team, the mind map (see figure 6.4) will help you to keep a high-level overview of what needs to be done and where you stand in the project.

Figure 6.4: a mind map

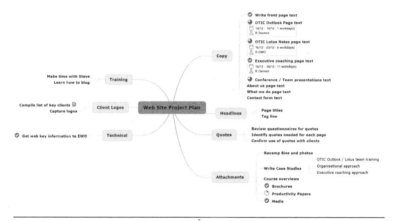

Mind maps are quick and intuitive to create, and make it easy to communicate complex information to others.

Use this technique alongside an Excel spreadsheet to plot the key deadlines in the project. (For a super-easy way to do this, go to the templates area in Excel and search for the project milestones template.)

Project board or work breakdown structure tools

As digital technology has evolved and our ability to share information online or in the cloud has grown, simple project tools have been developed, and these are gaining more and more traction in the corporate workplace.

If you are working on a simple project with many other resources, a planning tool such as Asana, Trello, Jira or MS Planner could be the perfect tool for the job. These *project boards* have been developed with simplicity and visualisation in mind. They are cloud-based tools, so accessible to everyone, wherever they are, whatever device they are using.

At the time of writing, MS Planner is a relatively new kid on the block in this area. It is a part of MS Office 365, so available to all Office users in organisations who have upgraded to the cloud-based version of Microsoft Office. Essentially, it allows you to create a simple project plan based on a type of project tool called a *work breakdown structure*. If you have ever seen an organisational chart outlining hierarchy within an organisation, you will know what this looks like. You can visually create workstreams or *buckets*, and stack the project tasks into each bucket.

Figure 6.5 (overleaf) shows an example of a work breakdown structure in MS Planner.

Figure 6.5: work breakdown structure in MS Planner

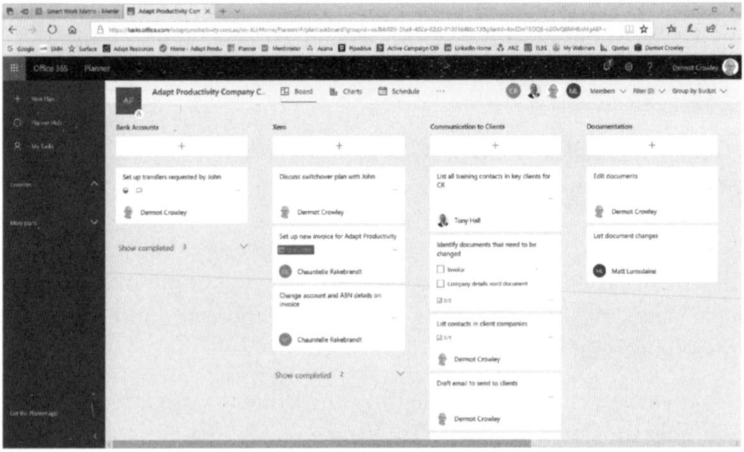

The power of these tools is in the fact that they are so accessible to the whole team and make resource allocation a breeze.

MS Planner allows you to quickly assign resources from your organisation to each task, and to communicate with team members regarding updates and changes really easily.

I mention MS Planner only because it is a part of MS Office, to which most people working in the corporate world have access. Other tools, such as Trello and Asana, are also excellent and very popular.

Checklist

If you have a simple project with only you or a just few people working on it, you may need no more than a visual checklist. You could create this on paper, but that makes it harder to share, so I recommend an electronic tool such as MS OneNote or Evernote. These are both excellent tools for collating and managing all your information, from meeting notes to research to project information. In the modern workplace, these digital tools can easily take the place of the traditional spiral notebook for capturing and managing information.

I use MS OneNote to plan many simple projects, especially when I am the only one working on it. I usually just want to break these simpler projects down into a list of things that need to be done in a rough sequence. OneNote allows you to create a checklist, with boxes you can tick as you track progress. It also allows you to send tasks directly into your MS Outlook task list, and to copy related emails from Outlook into the project notebook in OneNote.

The next time you are planning a project, think about using the best tool for the job. Don't just default to an Excel spreadsheet or a paper list.

Complex projects are easier to manage when you break them down into a simpler, visual format that can show you and others what needs to be done, when it needs to be done and what progress has been made to date. Visibility gives you control over the project.

Useful, usable and used

I have outlined a range of tools available to help us to manage our project work, as well as our day-to-day activities. But these tools are only of value if we can get everyone using them. If only a few in the project team adopt them, they will not aid collaboration. When everyone adopts the right tool, and uses it consistently, collaboration increases.

The challenge is not getting access to collaboration tools, but making sure they are useful, usable and used.

Our collaboration tools need to be *useful* — that is, they must add value and help us to do our job. They should also be easy to *use* in most situations. Finally, they should be *used*, not just by a few, but by *all* the relevant people in the team. That is usually where the value lies.

Let me illustrate. Last year we implemented a new CRM (customer relationship management) system in our business. I will be honest,

I have struggled with it. If I run it through my three criteria, I get mixed results.

Is it useful? Yes, it adds great value. Is it usable? That depends. If I am at my desk, yes. But if I am out and about, not so much. Access to the system from my iPad or iPhone is not great, and that is often when I need to review client information and input notes against a client meeting.

Is it used? Again, not really by anyone but myself and my business manager Chauntelle. Because of this I find it less compelling to bother updating it just for my own benefit. We are grappling with these issues, and feel there is value in doing so, but it has been a struggle.

Now compare that scenario with MS OneNote. I use this tool to take all meeting notes, to plan and manage simple projects, to collate research and even to manage my grandfather's historical records. I use OneNote every day, many times each day. I would be lost without it. Let's run it through the three criteria.

Is it useful? Yes, immensely so. *Is it usable?* Yes, it is very intuitive and easy to access on all my devices. Anytime, anyplace, anywhere as the Martini Rosso advert used to say. *Is it used?* Yes, the whole team has embraced it. In a few short months, it has become an integral part of our business practice.

Lead by example here. Don't expect others to do what you don't.

So how do we ensure that our collaboration tools are useful, usable and used? Here are some useful tips:

- Don't just jump at the latest gadget or fad. Take the time to work out what you are trying to achieve, and which tools can best meet your needs.

- Set the context with your team, and help them understand why and how this will help them do their job with a little less friction.

- Give them training so they know how to use the tool.

- Ensure IT have set up the tools in a way that makes them easy to use in every situation.

- Create champions who will carry the flag in the first few months. These champions should double as onsite coaches in the early days.

EXPERT INTERVIEW
Colin Ellis—on projects

Because projects are such a common way for us to cooperate with others, I decided to talk with Colin Ellis, a project management expert and author of *The Project Rots from the Head*. Colin has a refreshing and inspiring take on how to make projects more effective.

His first point is that projects are not really about project plans, schedules and risk documents. They are about people. This is often forgotten when planning projects.

> *It's a mistake that most project teams make, mostly because organisations tend to rush them through the project planning phase, or else a project manager has forgotten what their three jobs are. Their three jobs are to build a team, build a plan and deliver the project. I think when it comes to productivity in projects, you must start with a very firm understanding of what you expect from each other.*

> *Whenever I go into organisations to help them with their project management, the first question I ask is, 'Right, what did you do to come together as a team before you started?' Without that, you are going to struggle with productivity from the start because you won't understand everyone's personality. You won't understand the best way to get the best work out of them. You won't understand how to communicate properly. So we often start projects on the wrong foot. Building a team is the key to really, really productive work in projects.*

Of course, this takes time, and we are all under so much pressure that we may feel we don't have the time to spare. But I believe we waste far more time down the track if we don't do this.

Colin suggests that good project managers should develop what is called a project charter to get everyone on the same page.

Back in the day, we used to draw up what we called a team charter. *It was kind of a formal document, and a part of its value was that it outlined a set of working principles, what we expected of each other, and only once that was in place did you have a baseline from which you could move forward.*

As we have seen, projects are complex endeavours, even the small ones. I asked Colin for his views on tools to control the project.

It's more than just a Gantt chart. I always say to project managers, as soon as you start showing other people your tools you're really going down the wrong track, because they're only there to help project managers maintain focus and keep control of the project. The one thing people don't do regularly enough is gauge the happiness of the stakeholders. Stakeholders include the project team members and probably the person who sponsored the project in the first place.

The most important thing is to check in with the people. How are you doing? How are you feeling? Are you happy with the way things are going? What's one thing I could do differently? *Really getting what we call a health check of the actual team to see how they're progressing. Because as project manager, there are certain elements that are within your control, but most things are outside your control. Because projects are about people.*

You can't really control people. A Harvard Business Review *survey last year said that one thing people expected most from managers was the ability to inspire and motivate. And yet these are things we don't really capture in documents.*

Colin believes cultural change happens through lots of small projects—new projects every month to work on a different issue, or behaviour. Rather than creating a massive project to change the culture, take a more 'agile' approach and develop lots of small initiatives that work together to create change. I love this idea.

Finally, I asked Colin for his top three tips for managing projects more effectively.

> *First, really take time to get to know the team. I don't believe that as a team you can work productively if you don't understand how everyone ticks. Number two is to set expectations really, really well. Too often projects suffer from a lack of productivity because we haven't communicated the expectations in the right way. The last thing is as a project manager you need to stay on top of the work and drive for results.*

I love the fact that Colin focuses so much on the human part of project management. The heart of any smart team is its people, and we get the best results when we focus on the people as well as the work.

Urgency in the workplace often derails projects, and it can compel us to work reactively on projects when we should actually be proactive. It is a challenge I encounter often with clients who are involved in projects. In the following chapter, we will explore urgency and some strategies that might help to combat it.

7

KEY SKILLS FOR EFFECTIVE COOPERATION

'I don't think you understand, Dermot. We work in an industry that is highly reactive, and our clients expect us to drop everything when they contact us.'

A senior manager of a tech company put this argument to me quite recently at a presentation I was giving. Sadly, I have heard it many times over the past 20 years, from people in different industries, including technology, professional services, hospitality, manufacturing, retail, banking and government.

Everyone thinks their experience is unique in this regard, but I have found it is pretty much the same in every industry.

Urgency rules, everywhere.

This focus on urgency is a cancer that kills productive collaboration on our projects. I have seen a significant change in organisations over the past two decades. Everything has sped up. Urgency plays a major role in how we prioritise and manage our time.

Managing urgency

This urgency, and the reactivity it generates, derails our ability to cooperate in a productive way. In today's workplace, many of the poor behaviours that cause friction come from our, or other people's, failure to manage work in a timely way. So what has brought about this change?

One factor is that we are now working in a global workplace, with colleagues and clients in different time zones. This certainly has an impact on expectations and turnaround times. Another is the increased competition we face these days, which means any lack of responsiveness can undermine our relationship with our sometimes-impatient clients.

While both of these factors play a role, I believe the real driver is the rise of email and other forms of instant communication. As discussed at length in chapter 4, email has rewired how we think about the workflow across our team. We press Send and at some level expect an instantaneous response. At the other end, our colleagues are alerted that they have an incoming communication, which raises the level of urgency in their mind.

Add to this our smartphones, which keep us connected 24/7, instant messaging for the times when email is just too slow, and a social media culture that demands to be fed constantly. With all of this instant communication and gratification, it is hard to refute that we are bringing this urgency mindset on ourselves.

Most urgency is false

In *Smart Work,* I talked about the negative impact false and unnecessary urgency was having on our personal productivity. One of the key concepts behind *Smart Work* was working proactively instead of reactively.

At the team level, unproductive urgency is an evil that needs to be stamped out, as it destabilises our efforts to work together productively.

Some urgency is real, but much of it is false, which is to say someone else may describe it as urgent, or we ourselves may characterise it as such, but in reality it is not urgent at all. Email is a great example of this. Many interruptions also fall into this category.

Some urgency is reasonable, but much is unreasonable. Perhaps it is urgent only because someone else, or worse, we ourselves, left it until the last minute. Sometimes this is unavoidable, but often it comes down to lack of planning or proper prioritisation.

The pressure created by urgency is the cause of much of the workplace stress we see today. Workers are spending their days reacting to urgent stuff, instead of focusing on the important work that delivers results. Working reactively is like paddling against the current: we expend a lot of energy just to stay in the same place, making little or no real progress. Then we work on outside our core hours trying to catch up on our 'real' priorities.

We need to dial down the urgency if we are to work as a productive team. We need to minimise the unnecessary urgency we dump on other people's plates, and to learn to negotiate and manage urgency when it comes our way.

Reducing urgency for others

Reducing the levels of urgency our work creates for others comes down to one simple habit — planning.

When we take time out to plan, we open up the opportunity to work more proactively.

In thoroughly planning our week, we identify the tasks we need to delegate and we delegate these in a timely way. We think about our upcoming meetings and how we need to prepare for them. We think about our projects and what needs to happen over the next couple of weeks to drive them forward.

It is important to stop 'doing' and take time to plan, and to do this regularly. In my experience, most people get stuck into the urgent work straight away rather than stopping to plan. This is a false economy. You may feel like you are saving time but in the long run you will waste more time this way, for you and for others.

Work proactively

Qualities: *Purposeful, Punctual*

The antidote to reactivity is proactivity. Learn to manage and schedule your work in a proactive way, rather than always leaving things until the last minute.

Negotiating urgency

So what happens when urgency is foisted on you by others? How can you deal with this in an assertive yet diplomatic way?

You need to choose an appropriate response, taking into account the politics of the situation, the people involved and the consequences of your actions. You have four main choices:

1. *Ignore* false and/or unreasonable urgency. It is unreasonable to expect you to drop everything in the face of someone else's projected sense of urgency. In these situations, if you ignore them, they will usually sort it out for themselves.

2. *Negotiate* false and reasonable urgency. If it is a reasonable request, but you deem it not to be urgent, then you are in a good position to negotiate either when you will do it or whether you take it on at all.

3. *Question* real but unreasonable urgency. If it is truly urgent, but it is unreasonable that it has been landed on you at this late stage, you should question this, especially if this represents a pattern of behaviour. Set expectations for the future.

4. *Respond* to real and reasonable urgency. Okay, this is urgent and reasonable, so let us deal with it in a timely way.

Notice that none of these options involve the word 'react'? As you will see later in this chapter, *react* and *respond* are on the same continuum, but reacting should be reserved for exceptional circumstances that require you to drop everything.

Most requests can be dealt with using a timely response rather than a knee-jerk reaction.

As a manager, do you conduct or cushion urgency?

If you are a leader, then managing urgency is not just about your work. You also have a responsibility to your team to protect them from unnecessary urgency.

A part of your role is to act as a shock-absorber or buffer, to dampen the urgency being driven by other parts of the organisation — from senior management and stakeholders to clients.

This is a contentious idea, as many leaders conceive of their role as a conductor of that urgency. By communicating the urgency to their team, they ensure their staff get on with the job. In my view, more often than not this generates *senseless* urgency, rather than a *sense of* urgency.

Remember, in many cases the urgency either is not real or is unreasonable. Your job should be to evaluate this. If it is false or unreasonable, you may need to push back, negotiate or simply ask 'Why?'

A manager I worked with recently was an urgency conductor. Many requests and issues came his way from the leadership team in the organisation. He invariably passed these urgent 'crises' straight to his team, pulling them off whatever they were working on to address the new problem. His team experienced a state of constant anxiety. They felt they could never plan ahead, as their day and week were forever being rearranged at the last moment.

They were unconvinced that many of these issues were truly urgent, believing that other, more senior managers either defined them as urgent because that was how they got stuff done, or created urgency by delaying things until the last minute. The manager, responding to the higher-ups' seniority, let them get away with this, and expected the team to suck it up. Not surprisingly this was a high-stress, high-turnover team.

So what can you do to cushion the urgency a bit?

- Before accepting it, always ask when work is *needed* by (rather than when they *want* it).

- Push back on unreasonable deadlines.

- Make sure you know what your team have on their plate already.

- If something is truly urgent, ask why it is urgent. What could have been done differently?

- Fight to protect your team's time — it is their most precious resource.

- Remember, you are not working in an emergency ward (unless you actually are).

Be careful what you ask for

Qualities: *Purposeful, Mindful*

Think carefully about what you ask others to do. Make sure you really need it, and clearly outline how you want it done. Don't be the manager who asks for reports that never get read.

Developing an active mindset

As we have seen, urgency has a partner in crime that manifests itself in our behaviours — reactivity. We often deal with urgency by reacting. If reactivity is our preferred way of operating, we will always be less productive than we could be, feeling more stressed than we should, and a lot less satisfied to boot.

One way to recalibrate our mode of operating is to adopt an active mindset.

As you can see in figure 7.1, *reactive* and *proactive* are at opposite ends of the spectrum, with *active* occupying the balanced middle ground.

Figure 7.1: developing an active mindset

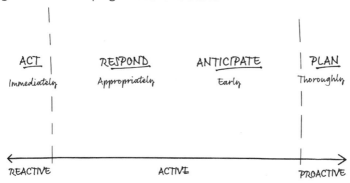

We need to be ruthless in evaluating incoming urgency. When presented with a task that is truly urgent and consequential, we should act immediately. But this should apply no more than 10 per cent of the time. Sometimes we should take time out to work proactively and plan thoroughly. This will reduce the incidence of unreasonable urgency for others.

I believe we should invest about 10 per cent of our time in planning. This will ensure we are focusing on the right work at the right time. But 80 per cent of our time should be spent working in the *active* zone.

Active has two parts, one that leans towards the reactive end of the spectrum, and one that leans towards the proactive side.

When I coach junior football, I always encourage the kids to be literally 'on their toes'. This means they are not sitting back on their heels, slow to respond when they need to move fast. They are ready to run forward, or pivot backwards, receive the ball or execute a tackle. Being on their toes is a physical stance as well as a mindset. Adopting an active mindset is like being on your toes.

Rather than simply reacting to incoming work or requests, an active mindset leads you to respond appropriately. This is a more thoughtful, timelier and more effective response that takes into account your current priorities and the opportunity cost of switching your focus. People with an active mindset are better prepared to go on the offensive. They anticipate early what is coming up, or what might come about, and they are ready for this.

An active mindset is a core strategy for dialling down the urgency across your team. It should become a part of the culture of your team, so you can say, 'This is the way we operate around here.'

This strategy needs to be led from the top, and modelled at every level within your team. It should become a part of the vernacular and be talked about in team meetings and in situations where reactivity is creeping in. 'Are we being active here or reactive?'

Negotiating our workloads

When we work in complex team environments, juggling projects with our day-to-day operational work, there is a risk that we can be overwhelmed by the volume of things we are asked to do. If we do not learn to negotiate, the quality of our work suffers, or we end up drowning and *we* suffer.

As leaders and managers, if we fail to hold the space for negotiation, we actually hamper productivity and effectiveness in our team.

Saying 'no' or 'later' is often a reasonable course of action, but we do this in a polite way, and base our argument on fact and careful reasoning. Saying 'no' because you are busy or you just don't want to do it is not good enough. But saying 'no' because the time expenditure would compromise a more important project, or because you are truly operating at capacity at the moment, is reasonable.

To say 'no' confidently you need to know your priorities, your workload and your limits.

Say 'no' sometimes

Qualities: *Purposeful, Reliable*

It should be okay to say 'no'—not all of the time, but sometimes, when 'no' is based on a reasonable conflict of priorities. Practise ways of politely but firmly saying 'no' when others make unreasonable demands on your time and attention.

Manage expectations using SSSH

In *Smart Work*, I talked about a strategy for managing expectations that I call SSSH. This is a great strategy for helping you to manage other people's expectations and to buy yourself some time. It works especially well with email requests:

- *Send* a timely acknowledgement.
- *Set* an expectation about when you could do the task.
- *Schedule* the activity so you don't forget.
- *Hold* yourself accountable for delivering or renegotiating.

I find the SSSH strategy makes other people feel confident that you will deliver as promised. It also dials down the urgency a bit and gives you breathing space to do the task in a timely way.

Saying 'no' requires a bit more thought. In a collaborative workplace, we don't want to create a culture in which everyone says 'no'. Nothing would get done, for goodness sake!

But when we do need to say 'no'. how can we do it in a way that does not cause offence, mark our card, or unleash World War III?

The first step is to acknowledge your appreciation that you have been asked to take on the project or task. They obviously feel you are capable and would add value to the work.

Next, politely decline the invitation, referencing your other competing priorities. This is a critical step because it makes it about conflicting priorities, not about you. It might look like this:

John, thanks for thinking of me for this project. It would have been interesting to be involved, but unfortunately I will need to decline at this point. My focus over the next few months needs to be on the new product launch, and I just don't have any spare capacity.

Sometimes there may be some negotiation around this. If the request comes from your boss, they may help you to reprioritise to fit the new project in. The key point here is that it is a negotiation, and this type of conversation should be encouraged. If we work in an environment where we have to do everything we are told without question, it will not serve us or the greater good.

Negotiating using the four variables

I often recommend clients use a well-known project management model that refers to the four variables in a project: time, cost, quality and scope. When one of these variables changes, one or more of the other variables needs to change to accommodate it. So if the deadline of a project is shortened, this variable can be accommodated by reducing the scope or quality, or increasing the costs to bring in more resources.

A client reminded me recently that these four variables can also be used as levers to negotiate your workload both on projects and in your operational work.

1. *When it is urgent*, see if they would accept a reduction in quality or scope to get it delivered by the deadline.

2. *When the budget is the issue*, see if it could be delivered later, or again, if quality or scope could be reduced.

3. *When the scope is increased*, ask if a bigger budget or more resources could be applied to the job.

4. *When the quality is non-negotiable*, is any movement in scope, timing or budget possible?

These levers offer creative solutions to get the job done. They should be a part of the negotiation and be used transparently to manage the complex dance that takes place in the modern workplace.

Hold the space for negotiation

Qualities: *Purposeful, Mindful*

If you are a manager or leader, part of your brief should be to hold a space for negotiation. Your team should feel confident enough to negotiate with you if necessary. And you should trust them to do this.

Delegating in the right way

When we talk about collaboration, we must also consider how we delegate work to others. A lot of friction is caused by managers delegating poorly and workers taking on delegation without asking the right questions.

In *Smart Work*, I outline a delegation framework that evaluates the experience of the person being delegated to and the risk involved with the work in question. Depending on the mix, we may take a *hands-on, hands-off, on-hand* or *hold-hand* approach here.

When delegating work, the key is to take the time to do it in the right way. That means we choose the right person for the job, and we take the time to plan and communicate the task so there is clarity around what needs to be done, and room for negotiation. We don't do this often enough, though.

As leadership guru John C. Maxwell puts it, 'Good executives never put off until tomorrow what they can get someone else to do today.'

We are busy and on the run, so we delegate on the fly. This often leads to mistakes and rework, so we are actually shooting ourselves in the foot.

The first thing to think about when delegating work is whether you are delegating a task or a project. If it is a discrete task, such as booking a flight, it is probably enough to tell the relevant person what you need, ensuring you provide clear detail on things such as dates, times and airlines. It is also a good idea to use an *if... then* strategy when communicating. For example:

> *I would prefer to fly Qantas. If Qantas doesn't have any flights available before 10 am, then check other airline schedules.*

This will save them having to refer back to you if your first choice is not available. The clearer your delegation, the higher the chances of success first time around.

If you are delegating a project, you really should meet face-to-face and plan the work at a high level together. Scott Stein outlines a great process for this in the interview that follows.

Delegate early

Qualities: *Purposeful, Mindful, Punctual*

Don't leave delegation until the last minute. This puts pressure on your team, and sometimes cuts off the options of delegation altogether. Be decisive and delegate work as soon as possible.

EXPERT INTERVIEW
Scott Stein—on delegation

As a manager, one of the common ways you will cooperate with others is when delegating work to your team. It is the manager's role to communicate and direct the work of others. Yet too often we don't do this well or, even worse, we don't do it at all.

I met with Scott Stein, who mentors senior leaders about strategies that reduce the risk of losing competitive advantage, talent and revenue. Among the key skills that Scott teaches leaders is when and how to delegate work. We started our conversation by agreeing that most managers and leaders don't delegate *enough*.

> *I think the impact of this is twofold. On one level, you have managers who are keeping their expertise to themselves.*

They might know how to do something, how to plan, execute, implement and deliver it, but the challenge is, those skills are not being transferred to the rest of the team. This also means the manager is starting to get overloaded and has less time to get their own job done. And quite often, it creates a disconnect with the team.

There's an opportunity that's missed for a staff member to grow and develop, be mentored and learn from their manager's expertise. Quite often that just won't happen.

One of the other challenges is that often delegation is left until the last minute. An email comes into a manager's inbox, but they have fallen behind so don't take action immediately. That email might sit in their inbox for a week or more without getting actioned. From there, there are two possible scenarios. Either they run out of time and realise it is too late to delegate, so they end up having to do it themselves at the last minute. Or they delegate it, but under pressure, which has a negative impact on their team.

They go, 'I'm going to put it off and I'll do it when I have time'. A couple of days or a week or a couple weeks go by and they realise they have no time to get it done. Then they delegate it at the last minute, which quite often sets up their team members to fail.

Not delegating work that you should can also have a negative impact on your own work. Every time you do something you should have delegated, you are not focusing on something that is a good use of your time. Scott has a great take on this.

One of the most common problems I find when working with an exec or senior exec around this is getting them to value their time. A lot of them aren't aware of how valuable their time truly is when they're focusing on the things they really should be doing to bring that business forward. Quite often they're getting involved in small tasks that are below their pay grade, but also below their thought grade.

Scott unbundled a four-level model for delegation that I think adds real value. At level four, the top level, a manager delegates without any real coaching or instruction, just an outline of what they want and a deadline. The mistake many managers make is they *start* at this level.

That can work with some people, but most of the time—let's say it's a new manager—they don't know about what you want or how you want it done. They don't know how you think. They don't have context for what you're really asking for, and quite often they are set up to fail.

If the delegation fails the manager gets burned, so they revert to level one delegation, where they don't actually delegate—they just do it themselves. This is what he calls self-delegation.

Scott reckons the best place to start a delegation relationship is level two, or what he calls a 'show', where you sit down together and map out the delegation.

I need some help with this. I think you've got the skills and capability to do it. Let's map it out. Here's what needs to be accomplished and we're going to work together on what steps need to be taken to make that work.

So I'm going to start by asking them what they think we should do, rather than just telling them. The challenge for a lot of managers is that they dictate the terms—you do this, then this, then this—when it should be more of an ask than a tell.

This very consultative approach to delegation takes time and effort, but in the long term this pays off. I see it as a 'game theory' approach to delegation. Over time your team will take on the new level of responsibility, and you will free yourself up to focus on higher level activities.

Scott teaches clients to map out the delegation visually with their team members.

Quite often I'll start with a sheet of paper. I'll put the task in the middle, then create a mind map, with arms radiating out from the central topic to the tasks or activities we could use to make it happen.

Scott then gets clients to move to level three, which is where your team members map out the task themselves, then check in with you. If you consistently model the mapping process, they realise they can actually plan it out for themselves and just check in to make sure they haven't missed anything.

Finally, your team can move confidently to level four, where you trust that if you delegate a piece of work to them, that they have the process, experience and skills to plan and manage it themselves.

This approach to delegation brings into play a number of the productivity values and outcomes outlined in chapter 2. You are delegating in a purposeful way, mindful of your people's level of competence and needs. You are helping them to become reliable, building trust and creating impact. A win–win for all.

So where are we now? We have looked at how to reduce the noise and to communicate with your team more effectively. We have examined meetings and strategies to make every meeting count. And we have explored projects and ways to collaborate more effectively on the complex work that really has an impact in your workplace.

You will have seen lots of productive qualities showing up as principles through these chapters, and I hope you are now excited about helping your team to work together in a more productive way. But where to start? How do you actually build a smart team?

In the final part of this book, we will explore some practical strategies that you, as a leader, can use to change the culture of your team forever.

PART III

BUILDING A SMART TEAM CULTURE

At the start of this book I outlined the steps to enabling productive flow in your culture. We looked at how to move up the ladder from distruptive to superproductive: *raise awareness*, *develop skills*, *champion protocols* and *inspire culture*. I hope you can see the opportunity here, and the way forward.

But as I have said before, I do not want this to be another book that you read and like (or not), but fail to follow through on. We need action! It is your job as a leader to inspire action and create momentum. And a few well-planned projects, executed with commitment and passion, are fundamental.

I believe the key to this change is creating simple, achievable projects that can be run alongside your normal work, then leading the hell out of those projects!

Peter Cook talks about the value of projects in *The New Rules of Management*. 'There is no magic bullet that managers can call on to grow profits, drive creativity, increase performance, lift engagement — or even give us world peace', he admits. 'But if there were, it would be implementing projects that matter.'

While many priorities will compete for your attention over the next few months, no one is likely to email you asking you to reduce the productivity friction in your team. This is a proactive initiative that needs your time, energy and focus.

The projects you create and run to reduce the friction may possibly have more impact on your team than any other projects you are involved in this year. They will make life easier for your team, reducing the stress and overwhelm they are likely feeling. They will improve morale as people feel they can actually make some progress on the important work they are trying to get to. And in this way they will improve productivity. For you. For everyone.

This final section focuses on what you need to do to create the change in your team's culture, and to sustain that change over time. Rather than embarking on a major organisation-wide cultural change program, I am going to suggest a more 'agile' approach.

Rather than trying to change the world, change your team. And rather than trying to change everything at once, implement one project at a time to build your smart team.

8

CREATING A MORE PRODUCTIVE CULTURE

How do we create a productive culture, where flow replaces friction? How do we lead our team into a new way of operating, and sustain the positive changes for years to come?

Even if you accept the challenge of leading your team into this new future, how do you overcome the roadblocks that external parties such as clients, head office, stakeholders and other divisions will build while you endeavour to make this cultural shift? They probably don't know or care that you and your team are on a journey to increased productivity.

Create ripples

If you are the CEO, or one of the senior leadership team, you may have the power and influence to create a change project that will have a positive effect on the whole organisation. But what if you are a divisional manager in a larger organisation or a team manager? What chance do you have of changing the wider culture when you are a small cog in a big machine?

As Stephen Scott Johnson suggests in chapter 3, you need to create ripples. Start with changes to your own team culture, and slowly but surely see how your behaviours create a ripple effect in the teams you interface with. Watch how your micro-culture influences the wider culture.

Create a micro-culture

I believe that even in situations where we cannot change the whole organisation, we can create micro-cultures that operate slightly differently from the wider organisational culture.

A micro-culture works in the same way as a micro-climate, which is simply a local set of atmospheric conditions that operate differently from the climate in surrounding areas. A micro-climate may be caused by factors such as a large body of water or area of concrete or tarmac, or even the slope of the land. Such factors can create different climatic conditions in that area. Ask a wine grower if their grapes grow differently on one slope or another, and you will find they know exactly where the best grapes grow. They understand the micro-climates in their vineyard.

Focusing on creating a micro-culture in your team, rather than feeling like you must change the culture of the whole organisation, will lead more quickly to positive results. And it is a much more achievable target. These results not only will have a positive effect on your team, but will begin to influence other teams around you as well. You may become the team that everyone loves to work with and aspires to emulate.

When dealing with personal productivity, the aim is to create new habits that improve our productivity. If we practise a habit consistently for enough time, let's say a month, we don't even have to think about it anymore, because it is just the way we now work.

A culture is just a set of collective habits.

When we collectively practise this habit over a period of time, we don't have to think about it anymore. *It becomes a part of our culture.* This is what we are aiming for with your team.

But what happens when you deal with people outside your micro-culture? How do you maintain and protect your productivity? You have different levels of control and influence with the people you work with, so you also need strategies in place to work with people outside your micro-culture.

Working with those outside our micro-culture

Working with others is a complex affair. We do not have much control over how anyone else works, and this can be frustrating when we are trying to protect our own productivity. So how do we implement the smart teams approach when we have no control?

Figure 8.1 illustrates a range of strategies that can be applied at different levels within your organisation, and even outside it.

Figure 8.1: strategies for organisational levels

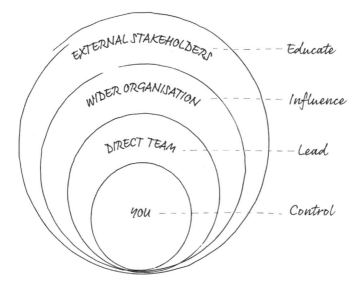

Control how you work

You can only truly control yourself and how *you* work. You can decide how you will organise yourself and how you will respond to others. In *Smart Work*, I outlined a system for personal productivity based on three core areas—Action, Inputs and Outcomes. How you approach managing your meetings and priorities is totally within your control. You can also decide how you will manage your own inbox, and you can choose how to achieve your outcomes. Take ownership in these areas, and make sure you have the optimal tools in place and the most effective work habits as a part of your arsenal.

Lead your direct team

The next layer out from you is your direct team. Whether or not you are a manager, you can show leadership here and lead them to greater productivity. If you are the team leader, you have the ability to introduce many of the concepts in this book, and to set up some expectations for how the team operates moving forward. In some cases, this might be by mandate, and in some cases by agreement. You cannot totally control the outcomes, but with work you can ensure that your team operates in a certain way, to certain standards, most of the time.

Influence the wider organisation

Once we move beyond your team, we can start to lose control and feel like we are at the mercy of a complex beast that cares little for our productivity. The bigger the organisation, the more this can affect us, especially if the company is multinational.

This is where influence comes in. As more and more organisations move away from hierarchical to devolved structures, the ability to influence has become an increasingly critical skill. We need to be able to get others to work with us in a productive way even though we have no direct authority over them.

Leading by example is the key to influencing the wider organisation. This means consistently demonstrating the productivity principles outlined in this book, and consistently pointing out when other people or teams cause friction for your team.

Setting clear expectations about how your team works sends a message and helps others to do the right thing.

Educate external stakeholders

So what about the people we collaborate with who are not even in our organisation? They could be clients, suppliers, project partners or many other types of stakeholders. The common thread is you need them to do stuff, and they need you to do stuff.

Often the key to effective external stakeholder management is education. This means helping them to understand the best way to work with you, and helping them to understand the benefits for them if they adhere to a systemised way of working.

In my workshops, I often hear the complaint that everything from the client is urgent, and the expectation is that you need to drop everything and react or you may lose the client. That sounds like a poor relationship that probably takes up more time and effort than it is worth. Time invested with that client in education can make life better and easier, even for the client. Of course, I am not talking about enrolling them in a course. I am simply suggesting that you have a conversation about the best way to work together and to build your working relationship.

The role of leadership on this journey

Matt Church, author of *Amplifiers*, suggests that leaders have only three roles. Firstly, to replace our fear with confidence they need to help us to feel comfortable and secure in changing times. Secondly, to replace our confusion with certainty they need to connect the dots for us and provide clarity. Finally, and most critically, to mobilise us in pursuit of a better future they need to get us moving and provide traction. If they fail in this last area, Matt believes, they are abdicating the leadership role. If you are a leader who would like to create a more productive culture, you must mobilise your team in pursuit of this better future.

Leading a productive culture

I once had the opportunity to work with the senior leadership team in a large consumer goods firm in Sydney. They were a business that was going through a lot of change in a competitive market and needed to sharpen how they operated.

The HR director was very excited about having me work with the leadership team to start with, then roll out training across the group once the team was fully invested and in a position to lead from the front. We locked in an initial date to work with the team, several months in advance because their schedules were so hectic.

A week before the training I received an email to say that the CEO had an important meeting coming up and would not attend, but the training would go ahead without him. This concerned me, so I suggested we lock in a coaching session with him to bring him up to speed. Without his commitment, the project was on a slippery slope to failure. Once this was locked in, all looked good.

But a week before the coaching our meeting was cancelled. Even though I was working with the rest of his leadership team, I knew that the chances of success had been dealt a real blow.

Sure enough, a few weeks later when I touched base with the HR director, he reported that a couple of the team had embraced their new way of working, but most had reverted to old, comfortable habits. He also recognised how disappointing it was that the CEO had pulled out of the training and the project.

To boost the productivity of an individual, you need to change behaviours. To boost the productivity of an organisation, you need to change the culture.

And this cultural change needs leadership. More than the support of the leaders, it needs to be led by example. Leaders need to walk the talk, not just expect others to.

A productive culture needs leadership. It does not just happen, and will not be sustained for very long without leaders making it a priority and consistently driving that priority forward at every opportunity.

It takes more than the boss's leadership, though. Of course, for success I believe that the boss must be not just involved but absolutely committed. But she or he must have leaders within the team who champion the new principles and behaviours, and keep everyone accountable. Those leaders may not have positional power, but they are influencers who can create change and hold a space for the new, more productive culture.

So what can leaders do to ensure the success of the project to build a more productive culture?

1. First, do no harm

Historically, all new physicians took the Hippocratic Oath and embraced the idea captured in the Latin phrase *primum non nocere*, roughly meaning 'First, do no harm'. What a wonderful concept to bring to leading people in our busy organisations: when it comes to your team's productivity, first, do no harm!

How often are those at leadership level the cause of disrupted productivity for the team? How often do we leave things until the last minute and end up delegating with urgency? How often do we call unnecessary meetings and invite more people than we should, just to be safe? How often do we request time-consuming reports that never get looked at, let alone actioned? These actions all harm the productivity of others.

By adopting a 'first, do no harm' mindset, we give our people a fighting chance to work in a more proactive, focused and productive way.

This is such an important concept for leadership that I believe every leader should have a sign on their desk to remind them of it.

2. Lead from the front

As discussed, leaders must lead from the front. They need to be productive, and be seen to be productive, because this inspires productive behaviours in others.

One of my favourite clients, a senior leader in Australia's largest independent home loan provider, shows great leadership in the area of productivity. Greg is young, very driven and a great leader of people. And when he comes across something that will make him a better leader, he commits to it 100 per cent. He does what he says he is going to do, and changes his behaviours when they are not as productive as they could be.

When I work with Greg's team, he turns up. Even though he is across the content and already applies the concepts himself, he turns up anyway. Because he wants to help lead the change that he expects from them.

As we cover new concepts, they often remark how they see Greg doing this stuff, and now they know where he learned the techniques. After we run training sessions, Greg ensures that he creates appropriate coaching moments with his team. He helps them to create the changes in behaviour over time, not just on the day of training. He turns up and he keeps turning up.

He does this because he knows that productivity is a leadership issue, and he knows that if he develops the right culture in his team, they will get more done in less time, and probably with less resources than they might like to have access to. They will also hang around longer as they will be more in control, balanced and feeling a sense of progress and achievement. It is such a pleasure to work with leaders like Greg.

3. Remember that you are always on show

As a leader, you are always on show. Every meeting, every delegation, every email, every lack of a response to an email, sends a message. And your team notice this.

I remember hearing a great story from a friend who had attended the Disney Academy in the United States to learn about their amazing customer service culture. One of the stories that had become legendary in the Disney culture concerned Snow White.

Apparently, there is a vast network of tunnels underneath the Disney theme park to allow staff and workers to get from one location to another without ruining the fantasy created above ground for the patrons. This means the kids see only the 'show' and not the behind-the-scenes stuff that makes the park run.

One day, Snow White (or the actor who played her) came out of the tunnel complex to have a quick cigarette. As she puffed away, a little girl and her family came around the corner and stopped dead in their tracks when they saw the little girl's idol smoking. The dream was shattered. I don't think that particular Snow White would have lasted in her role very much longer.

Remember, you are always on show. You, more than anyone, need to uphold your standards and live by the productivity principles in this book. Because no one follows a leader they don't believe in or respect.

4. Create projects for the team to rally around

Finally, as a leader, it is not enough just to inspire the team to make a change. You need to give them a practical and achievable way to do it.

The key is to create projects that will give your team something definite to work with, something to rally around.

One financial director I work with is a master at this. Whenever she wants to create a change, she calls it a project and rallies the team around it. This could be a new habit, a process redesign, an issue to be resolved or a report for head office. Her passion is infectious. Her team know it is important to her, and therefore probably a worthwhile endeavour. She will even give the project a codename to make it real, and to keep it top of mind for everyone it becomes a part of their weekly WIP meeting.

It is very easy to read a book like this, nod and grunt with appreciation at the points that resonate ... then do nothing. We can talk about qualities and principles all we like, but unless you find a way of bringing these to life in your team, reading this has been *informative*, not *transformative*.

Let us now look at a very practical way of creating the desired changes to your team culture. Developing a few productivity projects to run with your team over the coming months is the perfect way to put the theory into action.

9

SOME PRODUCTIVITY PROJECTS

In this final chapter I will introduce several projects that you and your team can use to quick-start your cultural change. My advice is not to try to implement every idea in the book all at once. Choose a project, and focus on that for a month. Then choose another project in the following month, and another in the month after. Over a short period of time your culture will start to evolve and you will become more productive.

Think of your projects as plates spinning on a pole.
Once you have one up and running, you can introduce
another, and keep them both spinning with
a little occasional encouragement.

Over three months, you will have embedded some simple but powerful changes in how your team operates. Not everything will stick, but if you take this approach you will see tangible positive changes.

As we have discussed, culture is just a set of collective habits. To change a culture, we need to get the team to do something collectively for a month, then build on this.

As a leader, you will need to champion these projects, and keep them top of mind for your whole team. As you demonstrate the required behaviours, you will need to hold yourself to the highest standards of accountability. And you will need to check in with your team regularly to ensure they are on track. This is more work to add to your overflowing schedule and task list.

No one said this was easy. Worthwhile rarely is, and this is so worthwhile. Now, to work!

The following is a list of possible projects that you could run in short bursts over the next few months. The examples are all related to the main three ways in which we work together — communication, congregation and collaboration. You could have one of these up and running tomorrow. Go on, give it a go.

Project 1: Productivity principles

How do you embed smart teams productivity principles within your team? Run a project to define and implement team productivity principles. To ensure success, implement this project over four months, focusing on a different theme each month.

Project purpose	To embed smart teams qualities and productivity principles in your team.
Project overview	Smart teams qualities and principles sit at the heart of this book. All of the tips and tricks and strategies introduced will count for nothing if you do not create a culture that supports productivity at a team level.
	This project should be the number one cab off the rank for projects, as it will create the foundation for all the projects to come.
Success strategies	The first activity is to bring together the team, or a select group of appropriate stakeholders, and to brainstorm the productivity principles that will address the most disruptive productivity issues you are facing.
	Next, communicate the agreed productivity principles to the wider team, and keep them top of mind over the next few months.
	Set a theme for each month over a four-month period, based on the four principle qualities—*purposeful, mindful, punctual* and *reliable*. This will help keep it at the front of everyone's mind.
	This needs leadership. As a leader, you need to walk the talk, rally the troops, and keep everyone engaged over the whole life of the project and beyond.
Stumbling blocks	You dictate the productivity principles to the team.
	You fail to adopt the principles yourself.
	Life gets busy, and the project is allowed to fall by the wayside.

Project 2: Interruption reduction

If interruptions are a major productivity issue for your team, consider running this project for a month to see if you can reduce unnecessary interruptions and increase focus.

Project purpose	To increase your ability to focus on critical work by reducing unnecessary interruptions across the team.
Project overview	This project should not set out to completely eradicate interruptions, but rather to reduce unproductive ones. It will require commitment from the whole team, and an understanding of both how they can reduce unnecessary interruptions for others, and what to do when interrupted themselves.
Success strategies	Firstly, as with the rest of these projects, clearly engage the whole team and communicate the project outcomes and benefits.
	This project could benefit from the use of visual aids to discourage interruption when someone needs to concentrate. Something that could be placed on their desk or the back of their chair will serve as a practical tool, as well as a way of keeping the project in people's minds.
	Identify spaces that could be used when people need to get away and concentrate.
	Think about ways to measure success. Maybe do a simple pre- and post-survey review of the perceived volume of interruptions.
Stumbling blocks	The problem is not taken seriously.
	External teams cause interruptions.
	No quiet rooms or spaces for concentrated work are allocated.

Project 3: Dial down the urgency

Run this project if you feel your team is more reactive and less focused on proactive activities that would reduce urgency than it needs to be. The key is to minimise reactivity by creating an *active mindset*.

Project purpose	To reduce reactive behaviours and create a more active mindset in your team.
Project overview	The aim here is to disempower the reactive mindset that defines everything as needing urgent attention. Your new mindset should encourage you to work proactively on important work while being responsive to incoming requests.
Success strategies	This project must be led from the front. Leaders in the team need to ensure they do not cause unnecessary urgency, and should protect the team from external urgency as much as possible.
	Discussing your expectations with the wider team is helpful. Holding the space for them to push back, negotiate and question urgency will empower them to have better conversations and make better decisions.
	Having regular conversations about external pressures being placed on the team, and brainstorming strategies to deal with these, will ensure the project is not sabotaged by external forces.
Stumbling blocks	Leaders fail to walk the talk.
	The team does not feel empowered to push back.
	Some team members cling to reactivity and urgency as a way of operating.

Project 4: Meeting diet

Imagine you had 25 per cent fewer meetings in your week. How much more stuff could you get done in that time? Of course, you should schedule meetings when they are really needed, but look to get rid of as many unnecessary ones as possible.

Project purpose	To reduce the number of meetings on average by 25 per cent across the team.
Project overview	Putting your team on a meeting diet should raise real awareness around how time is spent. Every meeting, and every potential participant, should be questioned. Is it necessary? Am I (are they) required to attend? Might there be a better way of achieving the outcome?
Success strategies	The first step is to review all regular meetings and question their value. Are they still required?
	A regular review of your schedule with your manager could identify meetings that might potentially be cut.
	You will need to keep a close eye on work progress and results to ensure that reducing the meetings is not impeding the progress of important work. Check too that your meeting diet is not frustrating other teams.
Stumbling blocks	Others from outside of your team are exerting pressure on you to schedule meetings.
	Team members are afraid to say no.

Project 5: Meeting agenda

Meeting agendas have been a part of the business landscape for many years, yet they are still used infrequently. The word *agenda* comes from a Latin term meaning 'things that must be driven forward'. Use this project to drive more things forward in your team.

Project purpose	To standardise the use of a meeting agenda template for all meetings.
Project overview	A great way to increase the quality of your meetings is to encourage the use of a meeting agenda template. It ensures good behaviours and increases the chances of your making the right decisions when planning meetings.
Success strategies	Delegate the task of designing a meeting agenda template relevant to your team's needs to someone who is good at making documents and forms look great. You will use it if it looks and feels easy to use.
	Set an expectation that this template will be used for all internal meetings, large or small. Discuss whether it should be used for external meetings or client meetings too. I think it is a great look, but you need to decide.
	Encourage your team to make the time to plan meetings then fill out the agenda template.
Stumbling blocks	Your agenda template is too hard to use.
	Some people use it and some don't.
	The template is used for only a few weeks.

Project 6: Turn down the noise

Email noise is one of the greatest drains on our productivity. It can lead to your missing important emails and feeling totally overwhelmed every time you open your inbox. This project can help you reduce the noise generated by your team, who are the people who tend to fill up your inbox the most.

Project purpose	To reduce the volume of unnecessary emails for each member of the team.
Project overview	This project requires every team member to be more mindful about how and when they use email to communicate, especially to other members of their team. Even a 25 per cent reduction of noise would have a great impact across the team.
Success strategies	A good starting point for this project is to set a baseline. Have team members count roughly the number of emails they receive each day over a week. They can then compare their results after a month.
	As a team, discuss alternatives to email and strategies that could be employed to reduce unnecessary emails. Discuss the use of CC, Reply All and email in general. Lastly, identify alternatives to email that your team could or should use.
	Try setting up rules in your email client to delete junk emails automatically and auto-file informational emails.
Stumbling blocks	You fail to set email expectations outside your team.
	You fail to review email noise periodically.
	Email overload causes paralysis for team members.

Project 7: Pull versus push

What communication tools do you have at your fingertips that you fail to use consistently across the team? There is an opportunity here to change how you communicate with your colleagues.

Project purpose	To identify and implement alternative communication tools to reduce the overuse of email.
Project overview	Your team probably have access to some excellent communication tools beyond email, but are not leveraging them. This could be because they are unaware of them, or do not know how or when to use them. This project could help to identify the most relevant tools for your team and expedite the team's use of them.
Success strategies	The first thing you will need to do is to work out what communication tools are available, and assess the pros and cons of each. You may have access to many tools outside of email, such as IM, Yammer, Slack, Enterprise Facebook or MS Teams. Review these tools and work out how they might serve your work.
	You will probably need to get some training on how to use the tools effectively, and to engage the team in using them. Don't skip this step.
	If you want the team to use these tools, you as leader will need to use them as well, and be highly visible in doing so.
	Find out if there are expert users of the tool in other teams, and ask for their help in getting your team up and running.
Stumbling blocks	You are not clear about how the tool can serve the team.
	You are not selling the benefits to the wider team.
	You are not providing appropriate training.

Project 8: The projects project

I love this one. It's about creating a project to improve your ability to manage projects! From my experience one of the most impactful things you can do for projects in your team is to increase visibility of project work across the team. So think about project tools now available that would serve the types of projects you are involved with. These include collaboration tools such as Asana, Basecamp, Trello, MS Planner, Jira, Confluence and, for simpler projects, MS OneNote.

Project purpose	To identify and implement a simple project tool that will increase visibility of project actions and progress across the team.
Project overview	If you currently manage your projects in your head, in a notebook or, at best, in an Excel spreadsheet, now is the time to upgrade to the twenty-first century. This project will give your team's work greater visibility, increasing your ability to manage project deliverables and deadlines.
Success strategies	One of the challenges here is that there are so many tools available now. Which should you choose? Talk to your IT department to find what is available to you. Chances are they are using some of these tools so could give you a quick start-up. Again, training will be critical here. Learn to use the tool, and choose someone in the team to champion its use.
	Start small. Don't set up 20 projects all at once using the new tool. Agree as a team on a couple of projects, and find your feet before you begin to expand.
	Be aware that no tool will offer a magic bullet for projects. You may still have to design a process to ensure next-step actions are actioned in people's schedules, for instance. This probably cannot be automated just yet.
Stumbling blocks	The team can be overwhelmed by too many tools—choose one to begin with.
	You are not regularly updating progress.
	You forget that projects are really about people, not tools.

POSTSCRIPT

So here we are, many miles travelled and many pages read. This book has hopefully provided you with some challenging concepts, some exciting ideas and some practical skills. It should also have provided an opportunity for you and your team. Let me describe this opportunity now by analogy.

There are two key ways that an organisation can increase profits. They can make more sales, and therefore more revenue, or they can reduce costs. I think of the personal productivity strategies outlined in my first book, *Smart Work*, as akin to increasing sales. They are practical strategies that you can implement to increase personal effectiveness.

Smart Teams is more like a cost reduction strategy. If you cut out the waste, the disruption and the friction, you and your team will save time. When you increase sales and cut costs, business booms. When organisations and teams both increase personal productivity and reduce friction, productivity booms!

I wish you the best of luck on your productivity journey. Do something today to start that journey—get stuck in. And get your team involved, because it will be they who build the culture you need to become superproductive.

As the thirtieth president of the United States, Calvin Coolidge, said 'We cannot do everything at once, but we can do something at once.'

What is the something that you will do at once?

INDEX

a**d**apt

Thank you for reading *Smart Teams*. I believe you should now have many practical ideas and concepts that you can take back into your team to build a more productive culture.

Creating a cultural change may take more than a book though. If you feel that one of our speaking, training or coaching offerings could help you and your team to implement the *Smart Teams* approach, get in touch through our website below, and let's make a time to talk.

www.adaptproductivity.com.au

I love connecting, so feel free to connect with me on LinkedIn or email me on

dermot@adaptproductivity.com.au

Until next time...
Dermot